BECOMING THE
FAMILY OF GOD

BECOMING THE FAMILY OF GOD

A Handbook for Developing Creative Relationships in the Church

Keith Huttenlocker

FRANCIS ASBURY PRESS
of Zondervan Publishing House

Grand Rapids, Michigan

BECOMING THE FAMILY OF GOD

FRANCIS ASBURY PRESS
is an imprint of
Zondervan Publishing House
1415 Lake Drive S.E.
Grand Rapids, Michigan 49506

Library of Congress Cataloging in Publication Data

Huttenlocker, Keith.
    Becoming the family of God.

    Bibliography: p.
    1. Church.   2. Christian life—1960–   .   3. Interpersonal
relationships—Religious aspects—Christianity.   I. Title.
BV600.2.H87   1986   250   86–9156
ISBN 0–310–75211–6

Designed by Louise Bauer
Edited by Anne P. Root

Printed in the United States of America

86 87 88 89 90 91 92 93 94 / 10 9 8 7 6 5 4 3 2 1

Contents

Preface

Imagine a church to which all of the members brought their luggage. Imagine, further, that no one was careful about where he or she left that luggage. Joe set his down right inside the front door. Mary took hers to the Sunday school class. Sue carried hers to the Women's Circle meeting. Bill dropped his in the board of elders meeting, and Frank took his to choir rehearsal. Meanwhile, Ted piled his atop the pastor's desk. What a mess!

That actually does happen. Each of us brings his or her *emotional baggage* to church. What sort of emotional baggage do you and I bring to church? Let's use our imagination some more.

Joe's baggage is his sense of rejection. It seems that no one has loved him very much. He is looking for companionship, and so he sets his baggage down right inside the door. There everyone who comes to worship will greet him warmly, so he thinks. However, when Dick arrives, he is running late, and so he steps right over Joe's baggage, just as though it weren't there. Now Joe feels more rejected than ever.

Mary's baggage is news that she may have cancer. She has come to church this morning ridden with anxiety. Scarcely has the roll been taken when she places her baggage on center stage. She needs reassurance. Unfortunately, the teacher, who has worked hours in preparation, sweeps Mary's baggage aside with a perfunctory "We will remember you in prayer." Mary feels that no one cares.

Bill's baggage is his anger with his boss. After being soundly berated Tuesday afternoon, he left the plant ready to quit. He wasn't going to take his baggage with him to the board of elders meeting that evening, but when Larry disagreed with one of Bill's ideas, out came the baggage. Bill was surprised at himself, and Larry had no idea where the baggage had come from.

Sue's baggage is the birth of a new granddaughter, her first. She bided her time at the Circle meeting to tell everyone. Over dessert she made the big announcement. Before anyone else could respond, Molly took ten minutes telling about her twin grandsons. After that the conversation went in many directions. Sue felt that her baggage was precious, and it hurt to think that no one else valued it.

Frank's baggage is his latent hostility over the bullish treatment that as a boy he received from his authoritarian father. Although most people don't know why, they have learned that Frank is "hard to get along with." Frank always brings his baggage to choir rehearsal. He sets it on the chair by the aisle in the third row (where the basses sit) and defies anyone to move it, least of all the choir director.

Ted's baggage is his felt need to protect the "status quo" at the church. He takes his baggage to the pastor whenever he sees a new idea coming or whenever he thinks new people are "taking over." The problem is that the pastor has an office full of his own baggage—his personal ambitions, his insecurities, tension with his wife, money problems, etc. Since there is no room for Ted's baggage, the pastor throws it out in the hall. What the pastor doesn't realize is that he has not seen the last of Ted's baggage. Ted will quickly gather it up and take it elsewhere—to the board of elders, to an influential member, or to a number of members. That's the trouble with baggage: it won't go away, and it just won't sit still.

You and I bring all sorts of baggage to the church—our hopes, our fears, our vested interests, our biases, our blues, our current turmoil, our unresolved "hang-ups," our schemes, our dreads, our desires, our obsessions, our confessions, and much more. The problem is not that we bring these to church, for that is where they belong. The problem is that we bring them unannounced, unlabeled, mislabeled. We are careless about where we dump our baggage. Conflict then develops when others handle our baggage in a way not to our liking. They are unobserving of it, disdainful of it, or threatened by it. They even pile their baggage on top of ours.

This is a book about baggage handling.

It is hoped that, in the pages that follow, you will recognize your baggage and, just as importantly, others' baggage. In addition, you may discover how to manage your baggage and that of others, even when it gets dumped inappropriately. As we become better at identifying baggage, learn to respect one another's baggage, and become skilled baggage handlers, relationships will go much more smoothly in the church. Since we love the church and derive a great deal of benefit from our affiliation with it, the unity of the church is very important to us.

Baggage handling is a big part of what being the family of God is all about. Scripture refers to it as rejoicing with those who rejoice and weeping with those who weep. We are specifically admonished to do that (see Rom. 12:15). Those who rejoice are easy to identify, but those who weep may not be. The latter include all the wounded souls among us whom we think of as simply disagreeable or temperamental.

Years ago I dreamed of writing a book about how to keep relationships in the church positive. That book was titled *Be-Attitudes For the Church* (Warner Press, 1971). Selected portions are included here, expanded by insights gleaned during the intervening years. Happy baggage handling.

Dr. Keith Huttenlocker
Anderson, Indiana

1
Getting Used
to the Family

Going together, enjoying the trip,
   Getting used to the fam'ly I'll spend eternity with;
Learning to love you, how easy it is,
   Getting used to the family of God.[1]

That is the way it is supposed to be in the church. And that's the way it often is. In a lifetime of association with various congregations, I have heard the church eulogized as no other organization or institution on earth. In fact, sometimes it is downright embarrassing to hear such profuse praise heaped upon a group of people who are, after all, only human. Can outsiders possibly believe the church is that wonderful? Maybe not.

   In my position, I frequently see the results of self-studies that churches make as a preliminary step in calling a new pastor. From a list of multiple choices, members respond to this statement: "The thing I like best about our church is. . . ." Survey results invariably show that, whether the church is large or small, the feature members find most attractive about their church is "friendliness." Surprisingly, this is true even when there is an element of conflict in the congregation. When asked to respond on a scale of one to ten (with one being low and ten being high) to the statement, "I feel loved and included in the fellowship of this church," the average score registered in most congregations ranges between seven and eight. If it is lower than that, severe internal conflict is indicated.

To me, this represents hard evidence that the church is, generally speaking, a good fellowship of which to be a part. Most of the time we can sing with enthusiasm, "I'm so glad I'm a part of the family of God." When God created heaven, He didn't reserve all of its joys for eternity. He gave us the church here on earth as a sample of the larger fellowship that yet awaits us. As we journey toward heaven, we are surrounded by brothers and sisters who nurture and support, confront and challenge us.

Most of us bring a lot of idealism with us into the church—partly because of our own notions and partly because of the way the church is promoted. We consequently expect our local congregation to be a kind of spiritual Camelot, where every man is a Dale Carnegie graduate and every woman is a candidate for the Miss Congeniality award. Experience soon teaches us that this is not the case. Do we then drop out, draw back, or develop some more realistic conclusions?

Naïveté can be deadly when it meets the humanness existing in the church. The challenge is to keep idealism and reality in perspective. So impressive were those first Christians that they enjoyed "favor with all the people" (Acts 2:47); yet their number included Ananias and Sapphira, a double-dealing couple whose profession was as hollow as a dead tree. Paul teaches us that Christ gave Himself for the church in order that it might be "holy and without blemish" (Eph. 5:27); yet the squabbling of two dominant women in Philippi caused Paul to write, "I entreat Euodia and . . . Syntyche to agree in the Lord" (Phil. 4:2).

In addition to being naïve, we may be too casual about our relationships in the church. We simply assume that, as the family of God, we are going to "live together happily ever after." We depend too much on traditional methods of promoting spiritual maturity, in hope of insuring unity in our

12

fellowship. If we go through the Sunday school curriculum, if the pastor preaches a well-balanced diet of sermons, and if our prayer meetings are fervent enough, we suppose that all our differences will be successfully ironed out. Experience refutes such conclusions. In fact, congregations that follow this pattern are often among those most afflicted with conflict.

A year after having helped a talented seminary graduate secure a pastorate, I was saddened by a phone call. "I feel I should tell you," the young pastor began, "that it may be necessary for me to leave here in the near future. I really don't want to, but. . . ." What followed was a depressing description of a small group comprised largely of older people with a long history of constant bickering. Since visitors could quickly feel the hostility in the air, the young pastor feared it was impossible to bring new people into the congregation.

We need to plan for unity in the church as intentionally as we plan for mission. The truth is that "getting used to the family of God" takes some doing. "Learning to love you, how easy it is." Not necessarily. Some of us are easy to love, but some of us are not. Getting used to some church people takes an extra measure of grace. Church members can be brash, brittle, biased, blundering, and bullheaded, just as non-church people can be. Simply because we find our relationships within a local congregation does not mean that we will naturally understand each other and easily accept our differences.

Proper attitudes and behavior are as essential within the church as anywhere else. In getting used to the family of God, the accent must be on *learning* to love, not on how *easy* it is. Rather than presuming that we will "hit it off just great," we must work at developing our relationships within the church. For two or more devout Christians to sustain and deepen their appreciation of each other, a growing process is necessary. God has graciously gifted us with the fellowship of the church; should we not be careful to be good caretakers of it? Are we not obligated to enlarge our awareness of the responsibilities that go with being family? To think it too easy could be dangerous.

13

If they are to survive the points of disagreement that invariably arise from time to time even in the best of congregations, church members must be supported by more than the initial euphoria of "pleased to meetcha!" They must be empowered by more than the momentary inspiration of a Sunday morning worship service. They must be deterred by more than a pastoral injunction equivalent to, "Children, if you throw sand in each other's eyes, you'll have to get out of the sandbox."

Those of us who share our lives together in the church must be informed about what *is* and what *is not* helpful to Christian fellowship. We are most likely to "enjoy the trip" if we are educated in how best to function within the believing community. Being part of the family of God is an art.

The apostle Paul recognized the effort required in order to have healthy relationships within the church. He offered this prescription: "With all lowliness and meekness, with patience, forbearing one another in love, [being] eager to maintain the unity of the Spirit in the bond of peace" (Eph. 4:2–3). We need to take his words seriously. They speak of the preparation of the spirit and the commanding of the will. Both are crucial to compatibility in the family. Many of our problems would not exist if we were more humble. Many of our problems could be resolved if we would simply determine that nothing shall come between us.

Beyond the gentling of our spirit and the girding of our will, however, attention must be given to the preparation of our mind. Too many times crucifixions within the church come from the same problem that led to the crucifixion of Christ—ignorance. "They don't know what they are doing," Jesus said. His tormentors were ill-informed about right and wrong. They were insensitive to the consequences of their actions. They did not understand their own human nature.

My observation over the years has been that most church people who act harmfully toward others do not take pleasure in doing so. They regret it. They are victims of their own "stinkin' thinkin'." They would delight to be shown a "more excellent way" (1 Cor. 12:31).

14

The good news is that unpleasant relationships within the church can become pleasant. Congregations with a long history of conflict can learn to live peaceably. Members who have kept the peace by enduring one another can come to enjoy one another. And good relationships can get better.

Twenty years ago, a strong church called a talented and ambitious young man to be its pastor. His future was filled with promise. Together they might have accomplished great things for the kingdom of God. However, it was not to be. Members of that congregation lacked understanding. They criticized their pastor, blocked his plans, and blighted his spirit. After a few years, he resigned, moved away, and went into business. In the following years, that congregation continued to make life miserable for its pastors. Its membership slowly declined. Although successive pastors may have contributed to the running conflict, the congregation, for the most part, earned its reputation as being a hard place in which to serve. There was no open division, but it was not a happy fellowship, either for its members or for its pastors.

Eventually, the situation became serious enough that members of the congregation grew alarmed about the future of their church. They knew that something must change or the church would die. During yet another pastoral search, a new organizational structure was introduced that provided an alternative to forcing a pastor's resignation when problems arose. A grateful chairman of the pulpit committee said to me, "Things are going to be different in the future. I wish we could go back and do the past twenty years over again." Hope now runs high in that place.

Pastors, as well as congregations, have much to learn about relating to one another. Pastors bring on many of their own problems due to poor relational skills and ineffective leadership styles. Sometimes when a pastor screams about how certain members have wounded him, he has actually shot himself in the foot. But that is a hazard of being a gunslinger. Good pastors aren't out "gunning" for anyone. They do not get hurt, because they are not trying to hurt others.

Before me is a letter illustrating what can happen when a pastor who is confronted with potential trouble keeps a cool head and a warm heart. The letter begins, "Since last I talked with you, God has been working some amazing miracles in the life of our congregation. One miracle that has opened many doors of possibility for our church was the successful conclusion of a two-year 'pioneer–homesteader' conflict [i.e., a conflict between the church's long-time members and the newcomers]. My ministry here is going very well." For those who understand why things go wrong and how to prevent it, as this pastor does, the family of God need no longer be viewed with suspicion. A sinister place becomes a sanctified place.

Getting used to the family of God is an adventure. We may never achieve perfect relationships, but we can make progress along the way. If day by day and week by week we are judging each other less and supporting each other more, if we are beginning to see through our brother's eyes and to walk in our sister's shoes, if anger is coming more slowly and forgiveness more quickly, then we may say that we are becoming family. One of the ceremonies I use in conducting weddings has this portion:

> Two people are not married in the ceremony of an hour. In these moments you are simply wed. In the distant moments known only to you and to God, you will begin to be married. Only in time, as you live together in intimacy and tenderness, will you become one.

So it is in the church. Only living together in love can make us into the family of God.

2
Building Strong Family Ties

One of the finest ways to compliment any established group—whether a work force, an athletic team, a club, a school body, or a religious congregation—is to say of it, "They are just one great big, happy family." We admire a group like that. We envy those privileged to belong to such a group.

How about the church at the corner of Main and Fifth? Is it accurate to say of those who meet there, "They are just one big, happy family"? That should certainly be the case! No group should be characterized by the quality of their fellowship more than the church of the Lord Jesus Christ. Even those who hated them had to admit that the early Christians loved one another in an incomparable way. The fellowship of the early church survived persecution from without and differences from within. There was no such love to be found among members of Herod's court, the Roman legion, or even the sect of the Pharisees. The early church *was* family—caring for one another, coaching one another, encouraging one another. Love and joy abounded.

"Just one big, happy family." That's my idea of the ideal congregation. Not that happiness is the only important thing in a church's life; but happiness is a vital ingredient. Good things happen when a congregation enjoys being together. Evangelism is easier. Enlistment is easier. Raising the budget is easier.

Worship is easier. Board meetings are easier. Breathing is easier.

Now we are not talking about a superficial, back slapping social club; or sentimental, toe-tapping religious entertainment; or issue dodging, ear-titillating preaching. But we are talking about the happiness that comes from the solid satisfaction of being an authentic, caring fellowship of people effectively on mission for God. That kind of happiness is contagious.

How can family solidarity be encouraged? How can a sense of community be created within a local congregation? These questions must be answered. Efforts toward solidarity and community need to be intentional. Too often it is assumed that if we meet together for worship two or three times a week, if the gospel is preached and we measure up to it, if all the tasks of running the church are faithfully discharged, and if all disagreements are quickly smoothed over, then we will have a quality fellowship. Not quite. It takes more than that for any local congregation to be "one great big, happy family."

What it takes may not even occur to us. That is because some of the elements are very subtle things—usually not programmed for. They may be outside the normal activities of the church and the particular responsibility of any single person or board. Some actually are provided for, but only incidentally. However, experiencing them feels good and the quality of the fellowship improves, even if only momentarily. Some are more evident in "high" churches; others in "low" churches. That, I suppose, goes to show that religious communions have much to learn from one another. If it is to enjoy a dynamic sense of togetherness, every local congregation must make provision for: celebrations, traditions, humor, and play.

CELEBRATIONS

Worship, of course, in its finest sense, is the ultimate celebration of the Christian community. Every Sunday morn-

18

ing the early church celebrated Christ's resurrection. Now, it seems, we only do that on Easter. But celebration should not be limited to worship, even great worship.

In most congregations some celebration takes place in connection with marriages, births, confirmations, baptisms, conversions, and healings. These are often too few and far between. Even when they happen they are sometimes downplayed, either because little attention is given them or because they are observed clumsily. None of these wonderful, momentous occasions should pass without the entire congregation participating in a sanctified "Hurrah!" If a celebration is allowed to pass, an opportunity for building family togetherness has been missed.

Beyond the usual celebrations, congregations need to look for other events of equal note and with equal potential for inciting happiness within the family. Early in my ministry with a great congregation we employed Lyle Schaller as a consultant. After spending several days with us and talking with many people (including nonmembers as well as members), he made two observations: (1) We did not do enough future planning, and (2) we did not do enough celebrating. To correct the former deficiency, we appointed a committee. Correcting the latter was more difficult since it required ongoing attention and fresh imagination. It was not that we lacked things to celebrate. It was just that we minimized the value of celebrations. False modesty also entered into the picture.

We were worshiping in a building valued at approximately four million dollars. Yet, the only thing we were aware of about that choice facility seemed to be how difficult the mortgage payments were to meet. When we arrived at our twentieth anniversary of occupancy of the building, we decided it was time for a celebration. Ladies in the church baked and decorated a huge cake, enough to feed a thousand people. We put it in front of the communion table. At the close of the worship the ladies cut the cake and the ushers distributed it so that every member had a piece to take home.

19

We had a wonderful time, shared a sense of accomplishment, and had a new thankfulness for what God has provided.

Another time the Family Life Committee, after devoting much attention to divorced persons, realized it was time to celebrate all the stable, happy marriages in our congregation. They planned an extravagant, elegant evening for married couples, billed as "Celebrate Your Marriage." Couples of all ages came, filling a beautifully decorated fellowship hall. Everyone entered by way of a bridged arch. After a delicious meal and delightful entertainment, couples repeated again their marriage vows. Why should not every congregation celebrate the fact that two out of three marriages make it? What is more worthy of celebration than a happy home?

The church held other celebrations: two for staff members upon completion of doctoral programs and one for a staff member and his wife for twenty-five years of service with the congregation.

Every congregation has things to celebrate and should take advantage of them. Don't wait until the hundredth anniversary of your congregation's founding. Celebrate something now, thus witnessing to what God is doing in your midst today.

TRADITIONS

Certain traditions are naturally kept in connection with the holy days of the year. It could be said that all the ordinances and sacraments of the church are traditions. For example, Jesus said of Communion, "Do this in remembrance of me" (Luke 22:19). Traditions are repositories of truth. They preserve revelations and events that could not otherwise be so vividly preserved merely through written or spoken words. They are dramas with eternal significance. A young man came to our congregation from a church in the "high" church tradition. He at once missed the colorful banners in the sanctuary that to him marked the several seasons of the religious year. That tradition had helped him focus on themes we seem to make less visible and, hence, less significant.

A number of years ago the congregation of which I am a member initiated a facsimile of the Passover meal as part of our Maundy Thursday observance. Thus, the circumstances of the initial Lord's Supper are re-enacted for us, making Communion all the more meaningful. This quickly became a tradition. After Communion we observe another tradition our Lord established; we wash one another's feet.

A church at which I preached once a few years ago had a tradition of holding a great Thanksgiving feast, with turkey and all the trimmings, on the Wednesday evening before Thanksgiving Day. (I thought it was a rather nice tradition, especially since I happened to be there at the time.) At one church I pastored it was a tradition to have an annual father/son banquet that was cooked by the women of the church. Not wishing to discriminate, there was also an annual mother/daughter banquet prepared by the men. Both were gala occasions involving hours of preparation and broad participation.

Not all traditions involve meals, ceremonial or otherwise. A fairly new tradition at our church is the annual "Hanging of the Greens" service on the first Sunday following Thanksgiving Day. It was an instant success, within the first two years outgrowing the smaller of our two fellowship halls, then the larger one, and finally being moved to the sanctuary. This is always a Sunday evening event involving all generations. In addition to decorating the room, there are songs and pageantry. The evening always concludes with hot wassail and cookies. Now Christmas would not be complete without this observance. What was once the mundane task of a few has become a blessing to many.

A tradition can be any meaningful experience. Any congregation can, and should, develop its own traditions. By them identity is established and heritage is perpetuated. Traditions are not to be confused with habitual ways of doing things. Unimaginative, rote patterns and practices should be discarded. Even some traditions that once held great significance can outlive their usefulness and should be replaced by new ones. Practices that can only be defended by such statements as, "We have always done it that way," do the family of God no service. Traditions are living ways of remembering who we are, whose we are, and from whence we have come.

HUMOR

Some people seem to think humor is out of place in the church. That is like saying laughter is out of place in the family. God gave us humor to lighten up our lives. Certainly it belongs in the church as much as anywhere else. Much of the humor on television and in the theater is either sick or vulgar. Let the family of God prove that humor can be used to edify rather than to degrade. Everybody likes a good laugh. God's people should not be deprived, and certainly not when they meet together. Religious meetings ought to leave us feeling better, and humor helps to do that.

A pastor should be a man or woman who laughs easily (but not insensitively), a happy person at heart. Even though I sometimes carried heavy burdens as a pastor, I felt it was important to share a few laughs with my congregation whenever we gathered (except, of course, for the most serious occasions). In fact, I never considered a sermon adequate if it did not produce at least one laugh and several chuckles, even if they came at my own expense. I did not usually rely on jokes, but on humorous stories or quips.

A few years ago our congregation invited the late Bob Benson to be a resource leader for the weekend. He often made us laugh, and sometimes made us cry. His humor drove home points that otherwise might have been missed—or resisted. Maurice Berquist, a communications specialist who once served as Executive Director of the mass media board of his church, is noted for his humorous sermons. Horace Shepherd, a black minister, has served a substantial congregation in Philadelphia for many years. As a young man he was promising material for vaudeville. Instead, he became a preacher. He did not, however, leave the funny side of himself behind. He brings lots of humor to the pulpit and is especially effective in speaking to young people. His sermons are forty-five minutes to an hour in length. Yet humor makes the time seem only half that long.

Humor in church must always be in good taste—not sarcastic, blasphemous, or off color. Timing is critical. The author of humor must be more than good *humored*. He must provide *good* humor. Humor does more than entertain. It creates a relaxed atmosphere in which people may feel at home. It provides spontaneity, a needed antidote to deadly formality. Where there is humor everyone is glad to be included in God's family.

PLAY

All worship and no play makes God's people a dull family. In the Old Testament the Israelites sometimes "danced" for joy. In the New Testament Jesus attended wedding receptions. Religion is serious business, but that's not all it is. Why should God's people not have a good time as well as spending their time being good?

Sunday school picnics and class parties are fine. However, if that is the sum total of a congregation's play time, someone is being shortchanged. Chances are that sooner or later those someones will look to clubs, unions, and other secular organizations to provide them with opportunities for organized play. When it comes to play, the children of darkness are wiser than the children of light. Wise up, family of God!

Every summer the men's organization of our congregation sponsors a golf tournament. They award trophies to the winning golfers and grill steaks over an open fire as part of the delicious smorgasbord that follows. Not being a golfer, I skip the links and head directly for the table (to fill the hole in this one). The men conclude the day with an outdoor worship service.

23

At various times in various congregations I have been entertained by an amateur magician, a singing sheriff, and a ventriloquist as I shared with the family of God in play. Members of those congregations have also done impersonations of Minnie Pearl, Jonathan Winters characters, and me. My assumption is that the family (of God) that *plays* together stays together—providing they also pray together.

24

3
Believer
to Believer

Luther said, "We are to be little Christs one to the other." This thought is close to the essence of Protestantism. The concept of the "priesthood of all believers" has even greater implications than generally given to it. It includes the individual's right and responsibility to search the Scriptures personally. It also includes his right to petition God directly without need of any mediator except Jesus Christ.

More than that, however, the priesthood of all believers recognizes the ministry of believers to believers. This does not preclude the role of the pastor. Rather, it supplements and is vital to the support of the pastoral function. Indeed, part of the pastor's ministry is to teach his people how to minister to each other, how to be "little Christs." This is spelled out clearly in Ephesians 4, where Paul says that God gave "some pastors . . . for building up the body of Christ, until we all attain to the unity of the faith and of the knowledge of the Son of God, . . . to the measure of the stature of the fulness of Christ" (vv. 11–13).

More and more the world recognizes the ministry of interpersonal groups. It is generally agreed that great work is being done today among alcoholics by Alcoholics Anonymous and other groups like it. The heart and soul of the AA approach is member boosting member. Psychologists know that a patient can go just so far via the counseling process.

Eventually patients must move into group therapy, where, in intimate communication with other troubled persons, one's true self is found as revealed through the eyes of others.

Long ago Jesus envisioned a great clinic of the soul and mind when He said, "I will build my church." To this day no other group holds such re-creative possibilities as does the church. For the recovery of sinners, God presents His redemptive team: the Savior, the pastor, and the church. Though the church is not the greatest of these, its significance cannot be overlooked.

The New Testament is replete with references to the ministry of believers to believers. "Look out for each other's interests, not just for your own" (Phil. 2:4, TEV). "Therefore comfort one another" (1 Thess. 4:18). "Teach and admonish one another" (Col. 3:16 KJV). "Consider how to stir up one another to love and good works, . . . encouraging one another" (Heb. 10:24–25). The congregation, peopled with little Christs who edify one another, cannot be other than a strong church. The quality of soul-care will make it so.

Those who think of the church as only a place where God is worshiped, or of a congregation as only those people with whom we worship God, miss the mark. This is as much a misconception as to say college education amounts only to what is experienced in the classroom. College education would not be complete without having a dormitory roommate, walking to class with a friend, cheering in the grandstands with the rest of the student body, participating in a rap session while drinking Coke at the student union, going with a date or spouse to the musical.

Nor should church membership be equated entirely with what happens between 10:30 A.M. and 11:30 A.M. on Sunday morning. Affiliation with the church is largely meaningless apart from relationships with the members. Otherwise, one merely belongs to the *organization,* not the *family.* Bill and Gloria Gaither don't just write songs about the family of God; they relate personally to those with whom they worship in the local congregation. The family of God has a sense of entity that lasts throughout the week. Conversations in the narthex, on the church parking lot, and over the telephone enhance and extend moments together in the pew. So do meetings of the women's society, the men's fellowship, Sunday school class parties, youth meetings, the visitation task force, and other structured or unstructured gatherings. Whenever believers meet, no matter what day of the week, it is a family reunion.

The ministry of believers to believers is at best unpretentious. Contrary to a pastor's ministry, which is of necessity weighted toward preaching, teaching, or counseling, brothers and sisters minister more informally to one another, often at unscheduled times and unarranged places. Though this ministry cannot be structured, it does lend itself to classification.

THE MINISTRY OF SUPPORT

This includes any caring that sustains another who is in need. Brothers and sisters need long hems on their garments. Within any fellowship of believers some are overtly or covertly reaching out for help at any given time. They may be going through deep trial, experiencing discouragement, or facing a challenge. They require "virtue" (strength) beyond their own, as did the woman with the issue of blood (Mark 5:30 KJV). Within the family of God are concerned, sensitive individuals whose radar seems to receive distress signals from those near to them. Paul reminds us, "Bear one another's burdens, and so fulfill the law of Christ" (Gal. 6:2).

27

Promising to pray for a troubled soul can be a significant form of support, providing it is not just a cheap way of discharging responsibility. Sometimes an appropriate verse of Scripture or a personal testimony may be helpful. At other times taking time to listen may be just what is needed.

I was once unwittingly involved in ministering in this way. I had intended only to join my wife in saying good evening to her supervisor. However, as we approached the supervisor's office we found her with another employee, who was obviously distraught. She welcomed us to join them. We learned that the young man's wife had left him the night before, declaring that their marriage was over. Barely speaking above a whisper, he poured out feelings of anger, anxiety, and guilt. His account was embellished with religious clichés and loose paraphrases of Scripture. We were joined by another employee, an older man who was young as a Christian. Eventually the four of us prayed for this grieved young man, asking God to sustain him and to direct his next steps.

Beyond giving encouragement, we may occasionally become involved in another's problem. If we can pour oil on his wounds, that is good. To get the hurting person to an "inn" is even better. For example, my wife offered our guest bedroom to the young man we encountered that night, thus hoping to diminish his loneliness.

Not all support relates to adversity. It can as well mean a word of praise during an "up time" as a word of promise during a "down time." Sometimes we may neglect such a word because we fail to understand how much it is longed for. A young minister bitterly complained to me that no one in the congregation had acknowledged a significant honor he had received. He is no longer in the ministry. Evidently the family of God blew that one.

THE SOUNDING BOARD MINISTRY

This ministry is for good listeners only. The approach is to let another bounce his thoughts off you—thoughts that may seem weird, carnal, or heretical, thoughts that are difficult to admit and that can be shared only with a few select, trusted friends. Such friends have the knack of listening with composure and responding with restraint.

The sounding board ministry is especially effective on behalf of those who need to ventilate anger, anxiety, or pain. Relief best comes when someone listens. The listener does not have to agree with a person's bias or to offer sympathy when sympathy is not justified. Nor should the listener be reactionary and condemnatory. What *is* needed is someone who will listen patiently and sincerely, who will give every indication of hearing but no indication of being judgmental. The disturbed person may not be seeking agreement or disagreement—only the assurance that someone knows he is hurting. Just having someone who understands and cares is of first importance.

The husband of a fine woman in a congregation I once served worked under a great deal of pressure and kept an impossible schedule. Sometimes when he was pushing himself too hard she would call me, ostensibly to request prayer. However, whether she realized it or not, she also released some of her own tension by calling. Rather than hastily tell her that I would pray for her husband, I listened to her blow by blow account of what he was facing in the next few days. I'm not sure he ever knew she called. That was not important. It felt good to know that I had ministered to him through intercessory prayer and to her through active listening.

A sounding board ministry serves those who have doubts. How else shall we come to faith if we do not address doubt? And how shall we answer doubt except to prick the minds of big brothers and sisters? Within the family of God there should never be a penalty for sharing uncertainty about beliefs others hold with certainty. Honest doubt is not to be despised, but discussed—in a reasonable, understanding fashion. During a Sunday school class, a searching young man admitted to having some doubts as to the existence of God. The teacher and a few other students pounced on him so vociferously that he spent the next two years defending atheism, a position he had not originally espoused.

Where there are those who will respond with active listening and thoughtful feedback, talking helps. It clears our thinking. It expels poisonous attitudes. It strengthens resolves. It separates fact from fantasy. It negotiates peace or organizes for combat.

Writing of the constructive interchange that should take place within the church's fellowship, Sam Shoemaker stated, "Here partial or distorted or even completely false ideas can come out, and find corrective—not from a leader declaring in dogmatic fashion what the truth is, but from the speaker feeling always freedom to say what he thinks, but then hear what others think. This double experience, of feeling that the group is going somewhere, and yet has time for mistakes and even at times the garrulousness of a newcomer, may work off more mental and emotional tie-ups in people concerning religion than reading a hundred books and listening to a thousand sermons."[2]

THE MINISTRY OF TUTORING

The ministry of tutoring is the ministry of instruction and correction in righteousness. Hebrews 10:24 urges, "Let us consider how to stir up one another to love and good works." Indeed, let us *consider* how. Otherwise, we may simply "stir up" one another. The Bible encourages "speaking the truth in love." It also establishes some strict guidelines for doing so. Colossians 3:16 declares, "Let the word of Christ dwell in you richly, teach and admonish one another in all wisdom." Galatians 6:1 requires, "Brethren, if a man is overtaken in any trespass, you who are spiritual should restore him in a spirit of gentleness." Being a spiritual tutor is serious business, not to be undertaken thoughtlessly.

30

    Whatever the perils involved, the ministry of tutoring is essential in order to move infants in the faith toward the stature of the fullness of Christ and to restore those who have begun to drift. Say, for example, we encounter someone who is verbalizing hostility toward the pastor or another member of the congregation. If, after a normal amount of ventilation, evidence of hostility is still strong, it then becomes the listener's responsibility to attempt the ministry of tutoring. In such an instance one might say to the agitated person, "You really are angry, aren't you?" Subsequent responses might be, "Do you feel comfortable with the way you are coping with this?" or "I hear a lot of bitterness coming out." The objective is not to condemn, but to confront the person with the seriousness of the problem.

On rare occasions a more direct approach may be in order. One day I went to our Rotary luncheon in a foul mood. I found myself seated with one or two persons who, it seemed to me, enjoyed privileged positions compared to mine. Between gulps of food I interjected several sarcastic remarks not particularly relevant to what was being discussed. Finally an old friend and good Christian brother looked directly at me and said, "It is unnecessary for you to be so negative." I knew at once his comment was in order. Making no defense nor any reply at all, I accepted his rebuke. Since then I have tried to avoid making that mistake again.

Sometimes the ministry of tutoring calls for a bit of coaching. Clarifying the norms of the family of God is a vital part of Christian nurture. The gentle persuasion of those who care for us as their own flesh is a rod and staff of comfort when we "go astray." When certain members of the Corinthian church began to practice gluttony and drunkenness in connection with the Lord's Supper, the apostle Paul found it necessary to warn them against receiving Communion unworthily (1 Cor. 11:27).

At other times older brothers and sisters may need to instruct younger ones in the doctrines of the church. Although Apollos was "an eloquent man, well versed in the scriptures," when that remarkable lay couple, Priscilla and Aquila, heard him preach, they detected some theological errors. Consequently, "they took him and expounded to him the way of God more accurately" (Acts 18:24–26).

Although there are times when private conversations with those who have erred are best, the ministry of tutoring often is most productive in a group. Just as the *family* of God is better able to offer support than an individual brother or sister, so is it often better able to give correction. A small group may be less confrontative and more persuasive than one person. For that reason, Sunday school classes, Bible studies, youth groups, and other small gatherings where there are continuing relationships and a high level of trust provide ideal settings in which to "speak the truth in love."

31

THE MINISTRY OF INTERVENTION

Any big brother or sister will usually come to the rescue of a younger sibling who is in trouble. In the family of God there is ample opportunity to practice the ministry of intervention on behalf of believers and unbelievers alike.

A reporter in our community decided to do a newspaper story on the inmate who had served the longest time at the Indiana Reformatory. Having identified the inmate, she arranged to interview him. The great iron gate clanged shut behind her as a prison official led her to the place where the interview was to take place. Finally she sat alone face to face with a convicted murderer. He was not a menacing figure at all, but a winsome old man who seemed utterly harmless. She listened intently as he told his story. For nearly forty-five years he had lived behind bars for a crime that he readily admitted committing. Moved with a Christlike compassion, she determined to seek this man's release. She appealed to a Christian judge known to be merciful as well as firm. The judge agreed that the man should be set free. Knowing it would be a sentence worse than imprisonment to turn this homeless old man loose on the streets, the wise judge said to the reporter, "I will grant the prisoner a new trial, providing you can find a home for him." Elated but apprehensive, the reporter set about to locate some of the old man's relatives. She found a niece in a neighboring state who was willing to receive him. The judge granted a new trial. The prosecuting attorney dropped the charges, and the man was released to spend his remaining years as a free man.

Jesus owned the ministry of intervention when He declared that He had come to set the captive free. He modeled that ministry when He came to the rescue of a woman caught in adultery.

The ministries of support, active listening, tutoring, and intervention are all ours to exercise as redemptive agents in the church and in the troubled world beyond.

32

4
Shaping Values

One function of the church is to guide people, individually and collectively, in the selection of goals that will bring the greatest measure of fulfillment in life. In the broadest sense, this is Christian education. Fulfilled people make a fulfilled church.

When my son was about eight years old, I took him with me on a trip downtown. We drew up at an intersection immediately behind a late model Cadillac. Not just an ordinary Cadillac; a Fleetwood. While we waited for the light to change, Marty said, "Wow! That lucky guy. I wish I was him."

"Who?" I asked, "the man in the Cadillac?"

"No," he replied, "the boy on the Honda beside him."

There is quite a spread of values among us. It has been said that one man's meat is another man's poison. We cannot understand another person's values until we have some insight into his felt needs. Jesus told a parable about a man's quest for a pearl of greatest value and another about a man's discovery of treasure buried in a field (Matt. 13:44–46). In each instance the man was willing to sacrifice all else in order to gain the pearl and the treasure. Each represented the supreme desire of his life.

With every one of us, our chosen means of fulfillment is to us the pearl of greatest price.

INFLUENCES

Our concept of fulfillment is influenced by at least three considerations:

1. Age. Values change with age because what might be fulfilling to a junior (i.e., a Honda) would not likely be fulfilling to a forty-year-old man (whose eye might be on the Cadillac). Felt needs and physical drives modify with age.

2. Our peer group. What appears to be fulfilling to our age group or social set usually looks good to us. If it brings our peers happiness it would do the same for us. Furthermore, if having that, doing that, or being that would enhance our standing with the group, we have an additional reason for being attracted.

3. Our assumed deficiencies. That area of life in which we feel most shortchanged is the area in which our values will tend to concentrate. For example, the girl who considers herself plain may disproportionately value beauty. We covet the pearl we do not have and take for granted all the pearls we possess. What we don't have—regardless of what we do have—makes us feel inferior. Any lack, keenly felt, makes us feel less than whole. It carries with it an element of stigma. Hence, we say of the great presumed equalizer, "If I had that, I would be happy" (fulfilled).

This happens not only to individuals, but also among whole segments of society. What was it that most disturbed the younger generation of twenty to thirty years ago? Poverty, with its attendant hardship and humiliation. So what are the treasured pearls of many persons now forty years of age and above? Affluence and status! What disturbs today's younger generation? A war that lasted too long, and parental demands that youth fit into a mold indicative of status. And so what are the treasured pearls of today's youth? Peace and individuality. The two generations don't understand each other's values. Ironically, both are seeking only what they have felt most deprived of.

34

Our values are compensatory. We choose the pearls life has not passed out to us. Hence, they often are selected out of negative motivation. Is it any wonder, then, that we are not very objective about them?

If we do not feel adequately gifted, our value system will be greedy, self-centered, and, likely, destructive. Our incentive will be to lay hold on that which inflates our opinion of ourselves. If we do feel adequately gifted our value system will be altruistic and constructive. Feeling no compulsion to compensate, we will be free to direct our attention outward rather than toward self.

We can live by positive values only if assured that "old # 1" has been taken care of. It is natural for persons who feel good about themselves to be unselfish, just as it is natural for those who do not feel good about themselves to be selfish.

The unhappy, unlikable, unsavory person is that way because his values are negative. He is ruled by his feelings of inferiority, which, in his search for equality, compel him to act in destructive ways: selfishness, intemperance, instability, self-pity, hatefulness. Sin, be it expressed as sensualism or secularism, is simply a misdirected attempt to find fulfillment. Sin is a perversion of a normal desire; often perverted because feelings of inferiority push the desire to lustful proportions. An inordinate zeal causes the transgression of a moral law.

Our problem is that we erroneously assess what will fulfill us. We choose values that minister only to surface needs rather than to the underlying cause of our discontent.

35

THREE DECEIVERS

Three of the biggest deceivers are materialism, popularity, and pleasure. All three seem to satisfy, since each appeals strongly to self and the self is all important to those suffering from feelings of inferiority. However, none of the three can satisfy. They treat only the symptom and not the disease. Because they do treat the symptom, they actually bring a measure of brief relief, like aspirin. However, the pain soon returns, and we either must seek another dosage, or another medicine. Blessed are we if we turn to that which is redemptive rather than that which only deadens the pain.

Remember, at least part of our value system is a reflection of our feelings of deprivation. The nature of the deprivation varies from person to person. Hence, when we are deceived about what is the pearl of greatest price, not all of us select the same false substitute. Things that deceive us by purporting to be the means to fulfillment are not, of themselves, wrong. They are wrong only because our sense of inferiority leads us to place almost absolute value upon them, to view them as being in themselves adequate to bring us happiness. Let us look more closely at the philosophy behind our selection of the three most common deceivers mentioned above.

1. Materialism. Materialism means different things to different people. To those who lack a feeling of acceptance it may mean the way by which acceptance is achieved. The reasoning is, "After all, I've done well. They have to acknowledge my importance." This is very typical of the delusion that money can buy almost anything, including acceptance. Or, again, still feeling rejected despite having done well, one may use materialism as a means to provide comfort in lieu of acceptance. To those who feel insecure, materialism will stand for security.

Whatever the felt need, materialism alone can't fill the bill. It can't buy acceptance. Comfort cannot suffice for relationships, and the person who is insecure isn't likely to be placated by any amount of savings.

2. Popularity. Popularity means just one thing to many of us: acceptance. The person who makes popularity the pearl of greatest price is so unsure of being desirable that mountainous evidence must be sought. There is a craving for more and more adulation.

He may want to be the star of the team. She may want to date every boy in school. Any symbol of popularity will be coveted. As we grow older, popularity contests become fewer. A middle-aged person can try to demonstrate his popularity by attempting to be the life of the party. (The person who *is* the life of the party without trying probably is not seeking popularity. He simply is secure in his sense of acceptance and, therefore, is free to act like a clown.)

Popularity, if we depend on it too heavily, fails to satisfy. A person can be popular without ever being close to anyone. The football star hears the roar of the crowd when he scores a touchdown, but who listens to him when he cries in the night over a broken romance? The detached person may have a lot of "friends," but few, if any, to confide in.

3. Pleasure. Pleasure, when sought as the source of ultimate fulfillment, means just one thing: self-idolatry. Pleasure as the pearl of great price represents acknowledgment of either rejection or failure. Out of friends or out of luck, there is little to do but seek entertainment. The logic is, "Since I can't find pleasure in relationships or in achievement (or both), I will make it up to myself by having as good a time as I can."

Pleasure, like the other two deceivers, cannot bring a lasting sense of fulfillment. We cannot live all our lives at the ball—and even if we could, who would want to?

When we seek satisfaction in wrong sources, we get wrong results. Not only do we miss fulfillment, but we often find our latter state worse than the beginning.

Jesus did not call the rich farmer a sinner. He called him a fool. He was, of course, a sinner, but only because he had been fooled about what would fulfill him. He could have kept on tearing down barns and building bigger ones and never been satisfied.

Our moods indicate our success or failure in pursuit of fulfillment. Often, the chronically critical person is frustrated in his search for fulfillment, and is out to punish others for it. Likewise, the despairing person has not found fulfillment, and is on the verge of giving up all hope of doing so.

We do not give up easily in our quest for happiness.

Most of us doggedly continue the process of buying and selling to get the pearl of greatest price and digging to unearth the hidden treasure. For us, fulfillment is just around the corner. We haven't achieved it yet, but the promise seems to be there. Again and again, however, when we think we've found it, we discover we have been deceived. Like the old prospector, there seems little for us to do but keep on looking.

The reason we have in our churches some of the dour people we do is because disillusionment has set in. This is especially true among the middle-aged. Many have never had it so good materially as they do now. Yet their nice homes and nice cars are hollow shells. These same people may have few meaningful relationships with friends. Perhaps they never did enjoy great popularity, or, if they did, dwindling contact has now largely isolated them. Disillusioned people are dull people. They are sullen, cynical, and sedentary. If their spirit is the dominating spirit of the congregation, it is not a healthy church.

The happy church family will be one in which positive, creative values are always exalted. Deceptive values will be exposed and "a more excellent way" will be presented.

38

PROPER VALUES

A few years ago the Gallup Organization and the Princeton Religious Research Center jointly conducted a major study of "The Unchurched American." The study seemed to indicate that the church is not meeting the expectations of either the churched or the unchurched. For example, to the statement, "Most churches and synagogues today are not effective in helping people find meaning in life," 49 percent of the unchurched respondents reacted with either strong or moderate agreement. Just what meanings do persons expect the church to help them find?

Spiritual

Surrounding spiritual values develop a faith system. The object in life is to identify with God, however one defines Him. One lives devotionally, that is, with his heart and mind centered on the divine.

To some the greatest spiritual value seems to be redemption. They cherish the moment when they were "saved," or, as some would say, "converted." At that moment they found "peace with God," and nothing before or since has ever been so important to them. Preached by Billy Graham and embodied by Charles Colson, the "born-again" experience is claimed by literally millions of persons in our country and around the world.

Some conversion stories are dramatic; some are not. A few years ago I met a previously miserable young man who worked in a brewery. In recounting his story he told me, "I had a terrible drinking problem. I didn't know I could be saved." His wife began going to Sunday school with their children. He would drop his family off at the church and then go across the street to play hockey. When his children asked him to attend the Christmas program at church he agreed to go. At the close of the service one of the leaders asked if anyone there needed to receive Jesus Christ as Savior. The man made no outward response. However, he did begin attending worship somewhat regularly. Again and again he heard the invitation to receive Jesus. He sat on the back seat weeping, still refusing to come forward. He thought he might be going crazy. Six months later, in the basement of his home he knelt down beside a chair and asked God to forgive him for his sins. His alcoholism was instantly taken away. So transformed was he that his conversion experience remains the focal point of his life. Without regret he quit his job at the brewery and took a menial position with a significant loss in salary.

Others who pursue spiritual values seem to place less emphasis on their conversion experience than on their daily

39

communion with God. I remember a radiant Christian woman who was married to a former alcoholic. She laced every conversation with mention of what Christ meant to her or what He had done for her lately. Her strong prayer life helped her survive the years when her husband drank so heavily.

For some the greatest spiritual value seems to be the assurance Christ brings. These persons have a strong faith system that shields them from stress and anxiety. Those of us who tend to be fretful find it hard not to envy others who are so confident of God's care for them. A retired church executive in our former pastorate, whose energy at eighty was as great as mine at forty, told me on several occasions, "Pastor, I don't know what it is to worry." His calm remained unbroken when his doctor told him he had terminal cancer. His only problem was he enjoyed life so much he was reluctant to give it up.

Still others depend heavily on spiritual values because of the sure hope of eternal life belief in Christ gives them. A saintly friend of mine lived with cancer for five years before death finally claimed her. During this long ordeal she seemed utterly fearless. A number of years before, her husband had died of cancer. His confidence became instilled in her. She was fond of saying, "He used to say, 'If I live I am the Lord's. If I die I am the Lord's. I can't lose either way.'" And then she would add, "That's the way it is for me."

To witness the joy and strength spiritual values bring to those who have them makes one wonder why anyone would settle for less. Other values are only so much tinsel and tinkle.

Relational

Surrounding relational values develop a support system. Some people carefully cultivate a circle of acquaintances to whom they are committed and who are committed to them. They live in community and delight in having friends.

Some value relationships because they fear loneliness and rejection. Perhaps as children they had no one who cared for them. They may have been only children or children of a single parent. It is as though their cup of fellowship was never filled and now they are insecure unless it is brimming over. A young man who is important to me has always had an almost insatiable appetite for companionship, first for that of his parents, later for his teenage friends, and now for his wife and children. He is much loved because he invests so much of himself in every relationship.

Some value relationships simply because they find people stimulating and enjoyable. I am inclined (at times, at least) to agree that, "People who need people are the luckiest people in the world." That is true if they need them for the right reasons. People who enjoy people have a high level of trust in others, although they are not necessarily naïve. They find it easy to be open. They do not seek intimacy in order to lean on others or to exploit them. They have no agenda for relationships except to give and receive according to the order of the day.

Those who value relationships for the right reasons have a strong fidelity to their friends. They assume servanthood readily. They are also comfortable when alone.

I greatly admire a frail but tireless man who values relationships for all the right reasons. He and his devoted wife have raised six daughters, most of them adopted. He has been active in the Boy Scouts of America and the Lions Club. He has cooked thousands of meals for all kinds of groups at his church. Meanwhile, he was a dedicated employee of a church publishing house, working for modest wages, going the second mile time after time.

The church is the ideal place to find relationships. There we find the greatest people in the world. As members of the body of Christ, we are related to a great host on earth and in heaven as well.

Philosophic

Surrounding philosophic values develop a belief system. Some people are deeply concerned with knowing. It is imperative to

41

them to stand on a solid base of carefully constructed fundamental convictions. These convictions may be moral, ethical, theological, humanistic, agnostic, atheistic, or otherwise. Whatever they are, they are the beliefs by which one is prepared to live—and die.

To one degree or another, we are all philosophers. If not, we are little ahead of the grasshopper. The psalmist was a philosopher when he asked God, "When I look at thy heavens, the work of thy fingers, the moon and the stars which thou hast established; what is man that thou art mindful of him?" (Ps. 8:3–4). The apostle Paul was a philosopher when he exclaimed, "Wretched man that I am! Who will deliver me from this body of death?" (Rom. 7:24).

Some give little thought to the "issues of life." Only when a major crisis comes, such as a threat to their lives or the death of a loved one, do they stop to ponder. This may be an indication of shallowness, or it may be an indication of hidden fear. They may find it threatening to contemplate philosophic values. Such values speak of accountability and of morality. By contrast some people devote so much of their attention to philosophic values that they seem almost immobilized. Important as are philosophic values they must not detain us from getting on with our lives. Many great philosophers such as Leo Tolstoy and Alexander Solzhenitsyn have been activistic.

Ultimately our only security is in what we believe. Materialism will pass away. Sensualism will fade away. Relationships will be taken away. "Those things most surely believed" are our last line of defense, providing we believe in God and also in His son, Jesus Christ. The apostle Paul had far more than question marks to stand on. His abiding affirmation was, "For I am persuaded that neither death nor life, nor angels, nor principalities, nor powers, nor things present nor things to come, nor height or depth, nor any other creature, shall be able to separate us from the love of God which is in Christ Jesus our Lord" (Rom. 8:38–39 KJV).

Thoroughly Christian spiritual, relational, and philo-

42

sophic values lend life all the meaning, direction, and security we will ever need. Such is the legacy of the family of God.

The apostle Paul experienced a revolution in his value system. This is his testimony, "I count all things but loss for the excellency of the knowledge of Christ Jesus my Lord: for whom I have suffered the loss of all things, and do count them but dung, that I may win Christ" (Phil. 3:8 KJV). Christ came to be the ultimate—even absolute—value in Paul's life.

43

5
Finding Fulfillment in the Family

Every one of us must experience three things in life in order to be fulfilled. To gain them is to overcome all sense of inadequacy and worthlessness. Now here is the important part: *These three can best be realized, not in direct pursuit, but as the byproduct of a redemptive, creative relationship with Jesus Christ.* And that relationship is begun and nurtured in the family of Christ's followers, the church. What are these three things?

1. We want acceptance. We want to be esteemed by others, to be taken seriously as persons, to have a place in the lives of others. Acceptance presumes a commitment from others; popularity does not. No one believes in himself until he is irrevocably convinced that others believe in him. Feelings of inferiority are rooted in the suspicion that the world (at least that portion of the world important to us) considers us second-rate by at least one of its standards of measurement.

Remember: our values are frequently compensatory, we aspire to that of which we feel deprived. Hence, if a person feels rejected, what will be his big ambition in life? To find acceptance, to win esteem and praise.

A number of years ago a very attractive young woman set her sights on Hollywood. Her ultrareligious and authoritarian parents seemed impossible to please. Feeling rejected, she set out to find acclaim as an actress. Tragically, her path did not lead to the silver screen but to a life of cheap harlotry. Deprived of acceptance by her parents and even the popularity she sought, she settled for the illicit love of a small time gangster by whom she bore a child who grew up to be a murderer.

We want acceptance. God wills that we have it. However, we do not find it by placing it first on life's agenda, but by turning our affections, full force, toward Christ.

When we do this, Christ brings us acceptance in two glorious ways.

First, He personally accepts us. His cordial invitation extends to all, "Come to me . . . " (Matt. 11:28). There is no greater feeling of acceptance than that associated with the experience of salvation. In Christ's great forgiveness of our sins we find overwhelming grace, and revel that we are embraced—vile though we may have been—by the eternal, omnipotent God, the most important being in all the universe. Imagine such standing!

We are accepted the way the prodigal son was accepted as he stood on the doorstep of home, enveloped by the arms of a forgiving father who declared to the rest of the family and to the household servants, "This [is] my son." What rank for one fresh from the pigpen!

We are accepted the way Mary Magdalene was accepted as she knelt at the feet of Jesus, washing His feet with her tears, wiping them with her flowing hair, and anointing them with perfume.

Oh, the exhilaration of knowing, "Jesus loves me! Jesus loves even me! Heaven accepts me." An endorsement like that makes self-acceptance possible. E. Stanley Jones writes, "Inferiority complexes, which are at the back of so much mere half-living are cured more radically by conversion than by anything else."

Unfortunately, many of us do not take seriously the flattery in Christ's forgiveness of sin. We do not take at face value the equation between the cross and what we are worth in God's sight. We are not overwhelmed by His grace, as theory discloses we should be. The tragedy is that consequently we do not experience full conversion, that is, we are not totally delivered from our hang-ups. Although our salvation is assured, we are not freed of our troublesome attitudes. We need another touch.

Secondly, Christ makes us acceptable. Although He can take us as we are, He does not leave us that way. He provides a "new birth." No matter what we have been, we can begin again, transformed into new creatures. There is no therapy for the human personality like spiritual regeneration. Nothing else can so drastically make the cantankerous compatible, the perverse pure, the fretful fearless, the haughty humble, and the unreasonable reasonable. No longer need we *feel* unworthy because no longer need we *be* unworthy.

A woman said of her husband who recently had been converted, "Two weeks ago I would've loved to have gotten rid of him. Now I wouldn't take a million dollars for him." That's acceptance!

Because of its strategic role in affording us a feeling of acceptance, the family of God will place heavy emphasis upon a personal conversion experience.

2. We want achievement. We need to feel that we have ability, that we are needed, that we contribute. For one person that desire may be satisfied with something as unpretentious as being a good pie-maker whose baking delights her family and friends. At the opposite extreme it may be something as outstanding as landing on the moon.

No one feels fulfilled until he can say, "I have been here and I have left my mark. It may not be a great work, but it is significant, and it is distinctively mine." Without that sense of achievement, he feels condemnation. Life seems worthless, and hence, as a person, he feels worthless.

The Ambitious Guest, in Hawthorne's story by that title, pushes back his chair from a hearty supper of bear meat and addresses himself to his hosts. His cheeks glow and his eyes flash as he begins to tell of a fire burning in his soul. "As yet," he says, "I have done nothing. Were I to vanish from the earth tomorrow . . . not a soul would ask, 'Who was he? . . .' But I cannot die till I have achieved my destiny. Then, let Death come. I shall have built my monument!'' The Ambitious Guest expresses for each of us the desire to achieve and to contribute.

We want achievement. It is part of God's plan. God said to Adam, "Be fruitful" (Gen. 1:28). However, when achievement becomes first in our lives, it becomes forbidden fruit. Being greedy for success leads to death. If, on the other hand, we seek Christ first, He leads us to achievement. When we set out to glorify ourselves, even if we reach the top rung of the ladder, we can only look out over our conquests and say in disillusionment, "Is that all there is?" But, if we seek first to glorify Christ, we can say with great contentment, "My meat is to do the will of Him who sent me."

Christ extends the greatest invitation to achievement when He beckons, "Follow me, and I will make you fishers of men." In order to contribute something that is lasting and of value, we must enlist in His cause, that of healing broken humanity through divine love.

Dr. Paul Carlson, a Christian physician and medical missionary, gave his life during the Congolese uprising in 1964. He was in the Congo by his own choice, because he found fulfillment in ministering to the jungle natives. When he visited there briefly in 1961, he wrote home, "It does something to you to work out here." Not long after, he volunteered to return. Why? Because Dr. Paul Carlson found a sense of achievement as a missionary that he never found in private practice.

In his early years, George W. Truett assumed the pastorate of a struggling Texas congregation. "I'll give my life . . . the best and all of it if need be," he said, "to make this into the greatest church in America." Forty years later when George Truett retired, he left behind the largest Baptist church in this country. That's achievement!

Is there any greater sense of achievement—no matter how meager the task—than when Christ says at the close of the day, "Well done, thou good and faithful servant"? Man knows no greater dignity than to be a partner with God, a worker together with the saints of all ages; to be able to say, I'm helping to make a better world.

Because a sense of achievement is so vital to individual fulfillment, the family of God will lay heavy stress on the importance of deep, personal commitment to the mission of Jesus Christ.

3. We seek autonomy. We want to be free to pursue our own course and to express ourselves in our own creative way.

To have a sense of identity we must establish and protect our powers of self-determination. Even as God instructed Adam to be fruitful, He also said, "and have dominion" (Gen. 1:28). A patient recovering from surgery once said to me, "After a while you get to feeling like you are not a person." Put to bed dressed in nondescript hospital attire, told when to go to sleep and when to wake up, given shots or pills at the discretion of the staff, confined, physically examined at a moment's notice, and too sedated or ill to have a will of their own, patients lose their sense of personhood. Their autonomy has been taken away.

The point is that something very similar happens when we yield ourselves to be the servants of sin. Nothing more degrades a man than to be ruled by a passion or habit over which he has no control. I have seen patients in state mental hospitals beg like puppies for their ten o'clock cigarette. I heard an old man tell at an AA meeting how, in his younger days, he would sell his summer clothes in the winter and his winter clothes in the summer in order to buy booze.

We want to be free. Yet when we place our desire to be free as the number one value in life, we become slaves. The secret is to reverse the process. As we make Christ the number one value in life—become His slave—then we are made free. When we accept what He says about sin and about

49

its power of enslavement, we are then ruled by a compelling desire to please Him, to imitate His sinlessness, and to seek devotional rather than sensual pleasures.

There is no greater form of self-expression than a life that is free in Christ to praise and serve God. There is no greater level of liberty than that of being free in Christ to say no to what one will and yes to what one will. There is no greater awareness of one's own identity than being able to say, Under God I rule my course.

The family of God will exalt the lordship of Jesus Christ, by which the divine will becomes the salvation of our own will.

6
Growing a Healthy Family

Every year hundreds of letters come to my desk. I observe that church stationery comes in a variety of styles. And with a variety of mottoes! Here are some of the ways by which congregations have chosen to present themselves:

"On Mission To Reach Out In Love For Jesus Christ"
—a small church in Alabama

"A Friendly, Christ-centered Church That Cares"
—a growing church in Florida

"A United Church For A Divided World"
—an Ohio church in a changing neighborhood

"We Strive For The New Testament Pattern"
—a black church in Kansas

One ponders just how accurate each of those mottoes is. What do they really tell us about a congregation's philosophy of ministry, about the quality of fellowship within the congregation, about the spiritual vitality of its members? Some are no doubt more descriptive of reality than others. For example, we may assume that the rapidly growing church in Florida is indeed "a friendly, Christ-centered church that cares." A friendly, Christ-centered church is likely to grow. On the other hand, I happen to know that the congregation advertising itself as "a united church for a divided world" has itself been painfully divided. The motto was adopted from a national religious broadcast, but the congregation did not live up to it when the pastor committed a serious indiscretion.

What, then, do these mottoes tell us? Only that we cannot adequately assess a congregation by what we read on its stationery. We must read further. Indeed, we must "read between the lines." Several criteria distinguish the healthy church from the unhealthy one:

OPENNESS VS. EXCLUSIVISM

Whether realized or not, whether a conscious decision or not, every congregation elects to be an open or a closed group. The two options are always available. The former choice leads to ministry, the latter to maintenance; the former to growth, the latter to stagnation; the former to life, the latter to death.

It may seem surprising that any congregation would choose to be a closed group. It is not surprising, however, when one realizes that the consequences are not usually so clearly stated. In fact, congregations make their choice based on considerations that may seem unrelated to those cited above. The choice is invariably determined by the congregation's understanding of its relationship to the society surrounding it. The issue is whether the church should exist in isolation from the world or in exposure to it. The choice is actually between one of two risks, for there is a risk either way. The answer is not best decided by choosing which is the lesser of risks, but rather by considering which risk is most imperative. It is quite possible that God demands that we take what appears to be the greater of the two risks because it also has the potential for the greatest rewards.

If one believes that the church must guard against the world's pollution at any cost, then he will of necessity advocate exclusivism. He is not likely to say so in any direct fashion. In fact, he may say quite the contrary. Yet, the caution he raises and the policies he chooses will nonetheless

52

make his position obvious. If he happens to be the pastor or a key leader in the congregation, he may solidify the choice. Little thought may be given to the long-range implications of that choice.

Negativism is prevalent in a congregation that opts for exclusivism. The preacher may sound like John the Baptist come again. Repentance is his theme when he is not otherwise lamenting the terrible shape in which both the church and the world are. Programs are minimal and ministries unimaginative. If the church launches any united effort, it is likely to be in opposition to something. (God knows there are plenty of things the church should oppose.) There will be little cooperative effort with sister congregations, except perhaps with those few who are like minded.

Progressive folk, of course, find it impossible to survive in such a negative atmosphere. Visitors, sensing the hostile environment, don't return. Young people drop out at the earliest opportunity. Meanwhile, the self-righteous, ever shrinking group clicks its collective tongue and bemoans the evil and indifference in the "modern world."

The alternative to exclusivism is openness. Make no mistake, openness is risky. History is dotted and the landscape is littered with congregations that opened their arms to the world and were swallowed up by it. The world is to be taken, not annexed. It is a mission field to be converted. The challenge for the church is to penetrate the world without being penetrated by it. In its openness to the world, the church must never sacrifice its own integrity. The only way to avoid this is for the church to instill within its members spiritual values and to teach them Christian doctrine.

Which stance Jesus advocated for the church seems rather obvious. He spoke repeatedly of the church's responsibility to penetrate the world. For example, He declared to His disciples, "You are the light of the world. A city set on a hill cannot be hid. Nor do men light a lamp and put it under a bushel, but on a stand, and it gives light to all in the house. Let your light so shine before men, that they may see your

53

good works and give glory to your Father who is in heaven" (Matt. 5:14–16).

Beyond these and other words by which Jesus contrasted exclusivism and openness, we have His own personal example. His style was always that of openness. Witness how He participated in a wedding feast, how He took His gospel to the wicked city of Capernaum, how He was accused of being "a friend of publicans and sinners" (Matt. 11:19). What does the Incarnation itself suggest but openness?

The open church is an exciting one. The mood is positive. The mode is receptivity. The emphasis is on possibilities. Redemption, reconciliation, and renewal are the watchwords. Rather than being stifled and ingrown, as is the case with the closed church, the open church seems to be self-regenerating since it is continuously infused by new life and new ideas coming in from beyond its own four walls.

Here on my desk is a newsletter from a growing, dynamic church whose pastor is a long-termer. What is the secret of this congregation's vibrancy? The most significant one: within the past six months the congregation has welcomed into its fellowship forty-four new families. Think of the energy and vision those forty-four families (probably more than a hundred persons) have brought to that congregation!

CHANGE VS. RIGIDITY

The long-range results of change are the same as those of openness. It must be said, however, that change for the sake of change guarantees nothing, except perhaps chaos. Change must be calculated and constructive. Change always, however, remains more viable than rigidity. The results of rigidity are predictable; the results of change certainly are not predictable, but at least they are promising. There is risk in change; but it is a risk our Master requires us to take.

Rigidity is the path chosen by the insecure. Indeed, one of the surest clues of insecurity is rigidity. A lack of self-confidence causes a person to place confidence in what surrounds him. The status quo becomes an idol. Change requires coping, and that is frightening. Many people identify with the church because they see it as a shelter from change, a bastion of the past. This is especially true of those who affiliate with conservative churches. Hence, such a church is almost predisposed to resist change. Rigid persons feel betrayed by the church when changes come.

Rigidity is not always the result of insecurity. Sometimes it is the result of simple conceit. Some people are so convinced that they are right they cannot entertain any new notions. They are almost snobbish in their attitudes, as though change were foolish, unchristian, or lacking in credibility.

Those who resist change speak much of the past, of hallowed doctrines, of ancient heroes, of sacred shrines, of established procedures, of reliable methods, of long-standing friends, of old professors, of yesterday's experiences, and of precious memories. Certainly all of these have their place, but they make poor proof texts when defending inflexibility.

I confess that, as a pastor, my attitude was invariably at its poorest when dealing with rigid church leaders. They frustrated me no end. (I hear more complaints about this from pastors than any other single thing.) Rigidity, however, is something I find within myself, so I must learn to be more tolerant of it in others.

55

Since conditions surrounding the church are always changing, it is imperative for the church to change, not in its fundamental character or essential beliefs, but in its methodology, its ministries, its staffing, and its organization. The challenge the church faces is to know what is timeless and what is temporal, what is timely and what is trite, what is spiritual and what is cultural, what is ageless and what is archaic, what is Scripture and what is sentiment. We have often failed to make those distinctions very well. Consequently, we have fought many a senseless battle. We must not exchange the faith once delivered to the saints for the fads often delivered to the secularists. On the other hand we must not mistake the family heirlooms for the pearl of greatest price.

Once the church has learned to distinguish between an idea whose time has passed and an idea whose time has come, it can face change eagerly and confidently. Jesus brought change to an uncommonly rigid religious community. As a result they crucified Him. However, the "new" idea did not die. It rose with Him the third day and has been an irrepressible force ever since, dividing history into A.D. and B.C., dividing God's covenant with His people into Old and New Testaments. We can never withstand God's changes. We can only cooperate with them or cut ourselves off from them.

Jesus clearly tells us that change must be accepted: "And no one puts a piece of unshrunk cloth on an old garment, for the patch tears away from the garment, and a worse tear is made. Neither is new wine put into old wineskins; if it is, the skins burst, and the wine is spilled, and the skins are destroyed; but new wine is put into fresh wineskins, and so both are preserved" (Matt. 9:16–17).

The church open to change is dynamic. Faith is exercised. Vision is encouraged. Creativity is celebrated. Innovation is welcome. The mood is anticipatory. Mistakes are permissible. Monday morning critics are silent. No dream is stillborn. There is optimism, but not foolhardiness; experimentation without recklessness; openness to expenditure, but fiscal accountability. Change should sometimes be undertaken slowly since, as someone has helpfully observed, all change is experienced by some as loss. Those persons will naturally oppose change. Yet it should never be necessary to either apologize for or defend change, since change is the price of rebirth and relevancy, of progress and potency.

CHARITY VS. JUDGMENTALISM

The family of God is a place of high expectations. It should be. If those who belong to the church are of no finer character than those who belong to the world, the church should blush in shame. In one of His most eloquent sermons Jesus told a great crowd of people, "Unless your righteousness exceeds

56

that of the scribes and Pharisees, you will never enter the kingdom of heaven" (Matt. 5:20). Remember, though, the scribes and the Pharisees were above average in their righteousness. Jesus' expectations are high! Unfortunately, where we find high expectations we also find judgmentalism. There will inevitably be those who fail to toe the mark, likewise those self-appointed persons who pronounce judgment upon those who fail. Some of us, unlike Jesus, have never been able to flank high expectations with charity. Jesus certainly did not condone adultery. Yet, He befriended a woman who had been caught in the very act. Jesus practiced charity!

Phariseeism was on its way out as Christianity was on its way in. The popularity of the New Testament church may have hastened the decline of the strict religious system that condemned Jesus as well as the woman taken in adultery. However, such judgmentalism had no future then, and it has no future now. Wherever it is practiced in the church you will see signs of death and decay.

Judgmentalism sprouts from legalism. Christianity gets reduced to a list of "do's" and "don'ts." Those who live by the list are "in" and those who don't are "out." Legalism assumes that since one is righteous in a few things, he is righteous in all things. There is little basis for such an assumption.

Judgmentalism emphasizes guilt; charity emphasizes grace. One assumes that we will do right only under duress. The other assumes that we wish to do right and are most capable of it when assured of acceptance. Someone has said, "You can't make seeds grow with a sledge hammer, no matter how hard you pound." Seeds grow best when they are fed and watered. That is the difference between judgmentalism and charity.

Charity sees the lack but does not require immediate perfection. That is why it suffers long. Charity is committed to individuals as well as to ideals. That is why it is kind. Charity remembers its own sins of the past and knows its own struggles in the present. That is why it is not puffed up. Charity gives transgressors the benefit of the doubt and assumes the best of others. That is why it is not easily provoked.

It is easy to practice charity when the sinner comes to repentance. "Now that you are sorry all is forgiven." It is not so easy to practice charity while the prodigal is still going his own way. Yet, charity is most needed when least deserved. Then it may woo us back into the fold, whereas judgmentalism will only drive us further away. We are told that "God shows his love toward us in that *while we were yet sinners* Christ died for us" (Rom. 5:8, italics added). In order to be redemptive charity must always be demonstrated in the face of sin. Charity is an act of faith as well as a gift of grace. If it is not timely, charity is trite.

If I cannot find charity in the family of God, then where may I expect to find it? Who more than the forgiven should be forgiving? Who more than the redeemed should be hopeful of redemption for others? Charity need not give permission, but it must give comfort. The family of God should be a shelter for those who are out in the cold of self-condemnation. Not everyone who is down on himself is down on his knees. Acceptance is no respecter of postures. Repentance always comes easier among friends than among judges.

Charity is not to be confused with tolerance. The world often gives tolerance to transgressors. If the choice is between the tolerance of the world or the judgment of the church, many an erring child will choose the world. He may even praise the world and condemn the church. Yet tolerance is *passive*. It never helps one see himself or to find his better self. Real charity, on the other hand, is *active*. Charity has as its aim the salvation of the lost. The family of God should always be an irresistible place to come home to. Charity puts out the welcome mat; judgmentalism locks the door.

58

HONESTY VS. HYPOCRISY

Not everyone in the church who fails to meet its high expectations can accept the rejection of judgmental people. They covet the fellowship of the family of God, nonetheless, and need the acceptance of church people. Only one alternative seems left to them: They pretend to be what they are not. For them hypocrisy is the only way to stay "in," even though they feel themselves to be out.

Hypocrisy, of course, is deplorable. It is demeaning. It is deceitful. It is damning. Sometimes seen as the lesser of evils, it may be the greatest of all evils, since it may keep one from ever becoming a whole person. In order to spare those who are weak from ever resorting to hypocrisy, the church must be a place of confession, a place where a person can own up to his sins without fear of reprisal. This is what God intended. James 5:16 declares, "Therefore confess your sins one to another, and pray for one another, that you may be healed." When we are free to confess our sins, we are able to deal with them. Hidden sins are protected from prayer. Confessed sins are subject to intercession. What joyous relief to be honest and open and to know that members of God's family still care about you and are actually supporting you in your battle to overcome those sins that have so long beset you!

Not all congregations offer that kind of caring. It is as if some churches have a sign over their doors, "Only the perfect may enter." Of course, those within are far from perfect, but all profess to be so. Dietrich Bonhoeffer said it aptly in *Life Together* when he wrote, "Many Christians are unthinkably horrified when a real sinner is discovered among the righteous. So we remain alone in our sin, living in lies and hypocrisy."[3]

Television glorifies sin, but the church often denies it exists. It seems, therefore, that wherever we find sin it is either covered with glitter or whitewash. Neither is right. Sin deserves to be exposed. If it is to be exposed in proximity to the atoning grace of Jesus Christ (precisely where it most needs to be exposed), confession must be practiced regularly in the church—and not just by the vilest of sinners but also by the vainest of saints! Bad people aren't likely to warm themselves at the altars of the church until a few good people have first been there to light a fire. Contrition comes forth most readily among peers, not superiors. We are all on this pilgrimage together, even though some of us have climbed a few more mountains.

The church must be careful to make plain the conditions of salvation. Moreover, the church must never be "soft on sin." However, in its zeal to be dutiful the church has sometimes been dogmatic. What was intended to be good has thus become evil. It is possible to so rigorously prosecute sinners that none will be found within ten miles of the church—at least not so far as anyone can tell. The church may presume that by stigmatizing the unconverted in its midst it invites their repentance. What happens in reality is that either they exit or go underground.

I once received a letter from a college professor explaining his somewhat rebellious attitude toward the church. The letter read in part,

> My own church . . . split several times in my youthful days—well, once as an infant, and again in 1930 as a 10 year old boy. It was the era of Billy Sunday. In our own church the pastor had the "saved" sit on one side, the unsaved on the other side of the church every Sunday morning and evening. So, very early, when I was 9, I got "saved" so I could sit with my folks on the saved side.

One must question, of course, how saved anyone is who makes such a profession merely as compliance to church protocol.

This church out of the past might be compared to a church of the present. I was called to preach to a congregation that was between pastors. The chairman of the pulpit committee was the worship leader for the evening service. As the closing hymn was being sung he left the platform and knelt at the altar. Taking over in the middle of verse three, I watched as others likewise came forward to pray. After a time of silence, the worship leader returned to the platform to conclude the service. Before doing so, however, he said, with dampened cheeks, that his own dedication had not been what it should be. It was a beautiful demonstration of humility as well as a courageous act of leadership.

These two churches vividly demonstrate how either hypocrisy or honesty can be elicited. Wouldn't you feel far more comfortable in the second than in the first? I would!

DISCOVERY VS. DOGMATISM

One of the most exciting Sunday school classes of which I am aware was begun by Dr. Robert Nicholson and his wife, Dorothy. Dr. Nicholson was at that time a college dean. The class was launched in an attempt to minister more effectively to young adults. From that day to this it has drawn a very diverse group. Many of its members are college students or alumni. A few have no college affiliation. Approximately half the members of the class are married, and ages generally vary between twenty and thirty-five. Members of the class represent many different points of view and lifestyles. Most have their roots in other places and come from a wide range of backgrounds and prior religious affiliations.

61

Curriculum for the class covers a smorgasbord of subjects. Use is made of college faculty and other resource persons. Given the composition of the class, discussion tends to be lively. Members thrive on testing their points of view. Each is stimulated by the others. In the process of defending their positions members gain new insights. In this class it is virtually impossible not to encounter some new idea and to begin processing it. The cross fertilization is healthy as well as enjoyable. The class is a welcome option to classes in which a teacher drones the "company position" while members either passively agree or inwardly protest.

What is particularly impressive about this class is the

fellowship among its members. Much caring is evident. Their discussions seem to bring them together rather than divide them. This occurs because of genuine respect for another's point of view. Dissent is permissible. Difference is acceptable. The class is an example of how a congregation can encourage the development of believers. Here again the vitality of the church is at stake as strategies and stances are chosen.

The church's concern must always be that people come to know the truth that can set them free (John 8:32). A corresponding concern is that the truth, or "the faith which was once for all delivered to the saints" (Jude 3), be preserved. To preserve the truth it must be imparted to members of the church. After two thousand years, the family of God remains the chief repository of any truth that expands on that recorded in Scripture.

The church is faced with a dilemma in its stewardship of the truth. If it clings too tightly to the truth, that truth is suffocated by sectarianism. On the other hand, if the church does not hold the truth securely, it can be lost through ignorance or apostasy. Time after time the keepers of the truth have made one or the other of these mistakes.

While a concern for preserving the truth is certainly valid, the point of emphasis is strategic. The church must forever be reminded that the truth exists for illumination, not idolization. The truth was made for people, not people for the truth. When that understanding is operational, individuals are encouraged to search for the truth and are supported in that search. When that understanding is not operational, people are simply *told* what the truth is and are restricted in their search for it.

With some guidance most people are eager to discover the truth for themselves and to apply it to their own situations.

The church with a future encourages personal search for biblical foundations. Indeed, the discovery of truth is something of a joint venture. All are learners; all are teachers. Denominational positions are secondary. Divine revelation is primary. Spoon-feeding is no more effective in the church

62

than it is in public education. Thinking people demand the right to discover for themselves what the Bible is all about. They are looking for quests, not creeds.

One young congregation has chosen, almost of necessity, an innovative approach to the Sunday vesper hour. The congregation, which has not yet called a pastor, meets each Sunday evening in the home of a member for an informal Bible study. Leadership responsibility is passed around. Several members of the congregation are well-educated, middle- and upper-middle-class professionals who do not find shallow and mundane sermons stimulating. They are, however, excited about what God is revealing to them through their Bible study together. A guest speaker is invited to fill the pulpit each Sunday morning and that very contagious service first attracts newcomers. However, the informal Sunday evening Bible study nurtures them into the fellowship.

The early church faced the question of how truth could best be preserved. Judaizers, who insisted that Christianity would have to conform to Jewish traditions, were the first dogmatists of the Christian faith. Others, like the Apostle Paul, contended that the gospel of Christ could not be contained by the law and the prophets. They invited converts not to circumcision but to circumspection. They were the first discoverers of the Christian faith. Had the Judaizers been victorious, the church might never have survived. Certainly it would not have come down to us as we know it today. We can thank God that Paul and his kind prevailed. The church in every age needs discoverers more than dogmatists, for no tradition—no matter how sacred—can contain all that God has to say to us with the marching of time.

INDIVIDUALITY VS. UNIFORMITY

The church not only faces a crucial choice in its approach to faith, it also must consider its approach to practice.

God likes variety. Witness the many colors in the world of nature and the vast number of species. God also values human freedom, for He provided each of us with a will of our own. Yet some churches give the impression that God has changed His mind about all this. Everyone is expected to believe alike, talk alike, worship alike, and maybe even vote alike. Uniformity is made the test of spirituality.

To be sure, there are some characteristics distinguishing Christians from the rest of society. "In Antioch the disciples were for the first time called Christians" (Acts 11:26). Apparently something about those early believers marked them as followers of Christ. But did that mean there was no room for individuality among members of the church in Antioch? No, for we understand from the Book of Acts and other New Testament passages that first-century Christians were quite different from one another. Imagine the contrast between Peter and Paul, between Barnabas and Apollos, between Philemon and Onesimus, or even between the sisters Mary and Martha. Not only were their personalities different, so also were their interests, abilities, and personal convictions.

Something about having differences seems threatening, distasteful, or even revolutionary. We may view fellow Christians who are different from us with either contempt or suspicion; contempt, because we consider them unspiritual, unworthy, unwise, ill-advised, or immature; suspicion, because we fear that their beliefs or behavior will replace ours as normative. Thus, powerful forces fuel our insistence upon uniformity.

What shall we do about this? First of all, we need to recognize why we are uncomfortable with another's differences. Is the feeling due to contempt or suspicion? Contempt may be hard to admit. Yet, we must ask honestly: Where is humility? Where is charity? Where is Christian concern? If our discomfort is the result of suspicion, what basis do we have? Many of our fears prove to be unfounded. Furthermore, the church belongs to Christ. It is presumptuous to hold ourselves singularly responsible for protecting it from all its foes.

We will live much more comfortably with the differences in the family of God when we identify our sources of discomfort and cope accordingly. It is unfair to force others to conform when their being different is our problem, not theirs. We may need to make the adjustments.

Obviously, some differences in the family of God must be addressed. Some actions are either so inappropriate or contrary to Christian values that changes must be called for. The apostle Peter could not accept the dishonesty of Ananias and Sapphira. Paul could not accept the immorality of a member of the church in Corinth who reportedly had taken his father's wife. However, our intolerance of lesser differences must be questioned. Such intolerance needlessly divides us. It is more accurately attributed to childishness than to righteousness.

Forced conformity stifles those who are subjected to it and repels those who refuse to be subjected to it. Furthermore, uniformity is suffocating to the group that demands it. Making allowance for individuality dignifies each member of God's family. In turn, the unique presence and perspective of each individual enriches the group.

The dynamic church will not be devoid of convictions. To the contrary, it will hold firmly to authentic theological beliefs and Christian standards. These beliefs and standards will be authentic because each person will have forged his own. Faith and practice will have been tried by fire. There will be no robots reciting rote answers. Free to agree or disagree, all will have had to give a reason for the hope that is within them (1 Peter 3:15).

The church should be the community in which people can find themselves. This applies whether one is a young person or simply young in Christian faith. Each of us needs to discover those meanings in life that distinguish us as moral and religious beings. Until we know what we believe, we cannot know who we are or have any sense of entity.

When the church pushes too hard for quick uniformity, the process of finding oneself is often aborted. A person who begins to think for himself senses the disapproval of such a church. The church becomes anxious about him and about his influence on the group. James Dolby writes of the squeeze in which the questing Christian finds himself:

> The pressures from without may be fatal; they may destroy the possibility of self-discovery or personal honesty. They may press in till one gasps for air and pleads for mercy. I can hear the voices of the pressures from without—"Have you changed?" "We understand you." "You had better be more careful." "Don't be naïve." "How could you say that and be truly Christian?" "He must be having difficulties in his spiritual life." Often at this point people give up the task of self-discovery. These pressures are too great. We are inadequate to break through the walls of protection and provincialism. We have lost ourselves in all our complexity.[4]

The second mistake the church may make is to offer the lost no guidance at all, to stand back and say, "Grope around for yourself. One way is as good as another." This leaves the seeker with no assurance of ever coming to an abiding belief. The expectation that one can become rooted and grounded in truth without ever being told what is truth is an absurdity. Freedom of thought is to be encouraged only if with it a sound biblical basis is provided upon which convictions can be formed. Otherwise, chaos will result.

The church must speak with surety but without intimidation. Firm positions are more helpful than detrimental *providing* the emphasis is on the Word, not on the offender. Let the gospel, not the preacher be personal. The relevant church does not rebuke as Jesus rebuked the Devil in the wilderness, but as He took a little child and set him in the midst of them. Laying it on the line can be an act of rejection or an act of redemption. The focal point makes the difference.

7
Understanding Family Members

I was leading a small group discussion as part of an in-service training program for ministers. "I have a problem," said a pastor, his face a study in earnestness. The problem involved a member of his congregation, a middle-aged woman who over a number of years had terrorized each of his predecessors and was even now making life extremely difficult for him.

Nor was the woman's divisiveness confined to the local scene, for the pastor was particularly grieved over this woman's reported verbal attack on the leader of a recent Christian education convention. "What can I do?" he asked despairingly. Within a few months he was gone, handing on the problem to his successor. He left an unhappy church behind but he also was unhappy.

Assuming this report was valid (and the man's reputation and record lead me to believe it was), this situation and others of which it is typical are altogether unbecoming to any group purporting to represent Jesus Christ. Yet the question persists: What can be done?

Although they parade under a variety of guises, the great majority of church schisms stem from a conflict of opinion or from a clash of personalities. Usually these involve the pastor and one or more laymen in the church. In almost every instance, at least one of the persons involved is maladjusted to some degree. The pastor is often at fault. Because of his own hang-ups, he precipitates problems, or at least substantially contributes to them. By his own reactionary attitude, the pastor can aggravate a situation that would have passed without a ripple, had it been handled with discretion.

But let us be fair. Not all church problems are preacher problems. In many cases, such as in the one just given, trouble originates with a disturbed layman who strains relationship after relationship, time after time, despite the exercise of patience and wisdom by the pastor. We shall not have happy churches until we acquire the means to cope with these inwardly wretched persons who chronically disrupt the peace of local congregations.

How ironic that blatant displays of carnality should occur within the religious community! One would certainly not deny the hymnwriter's assertion that there is "power in the blood to save from sin, to bring the peace of God where guilt hath been," but experience tells us that many a man who claims to be "saved and sanctified" is nonetheless a genuine thorn in the side of his pastor and many other members in the church.

It seems to me that many people experience only partial conversion. They are like the blind man of Bethsaida who after Jesus' first touch said, "I see men as trees walking." Some people require the second touch of pastoral (and perhaps even medical) care if they are ever to be made whole.

Some bad habits are eliminated and some words are dropped from their vocabulary. However, their attitudes remain essentially unchanged. Brought into the fellowship of the church, those attitudes pose a challenge for the rest of the family. It is easy to think less of the church because of the presence of such people. Instead, we should attempt to feel what they feel; to discover how they think. Only then can we prevent or resolve the problems they cause.

Disagreeable people speak and act as they do for a reason. Out of all the relationships they have experienced during their formative years, and usually in reaction to the pain associated with one or two highly significant relation-

68

ships, they have developed their own unique coping systems. They have learned to survive, or to get their own way, or to get attention, or to get even. To understand their sense of rejection is to feel empathy rather than contempt for them.

Labeling and libeling church irritants will not change them. Understanding and loving them may. Some can be loved out of their meanness. Others can be retrained. A few will just have to be accepted "as is." Beyond understanding and loving them, we must also learn how best to function in relationship with them. It may be more possible to live peaceably with them than we have thought.

I pastored for too many years before realizing that not everyone responds to the same treatment. Psychologists tell us that there are approximately seven different personality types, each requiring a particular kind of care in order to stimulate the most effective relationship. A pastor needs to know whom to treat with firmness, whom he must shower with love and attention, whom he must allow to lean on him, and whom he must not allow to lean on him. He needs to know who will want to be approached cautiously and who will want an overt approach.

Lyle had been a backslider for years. He was in poor health and often in the hospital. Each time, he welcomed my prayers, but he never came to church after being discharged. Finally, I said to him on one of my visits, "If I had as much wrong with me as you have, I wouldn't waste five minutes away from God." It worked! In two weeks Lyle was in church, and in a month he was converted. He has been an inspiring example to us ever since.

Armanda was elusive when she first started attending our church. Although pleasant, she would not permit better acquaintance. After she had come regularly for several weeks, I invited her to participate in a fellowship time for people new to our congregation. She declined and was absent the next three Sundays. I sensed that we had gotten too close and did not pursue the contact. Finally, she phoned and asked to see me at once. I was not available, but returned her call as soon as possible and made an appointment for later in the week.

Just as I expected, she phoned the day prior and canceled her appointment. I did not push, but assured her of my continuing concern. The following Wednesday evening, she asked to see me at the close of prayer service. At that time, she shared freely her problems and closed out the interview by inviting Christ to become her Savior. Two entirely different approaches to two entirely different types of personalities. That's all a part of being the family of God.

As with shovels, so with people—it is important to take hold of them at the right end. The key is to find the handle, not the blade. Most of us tend to relate to others out of a single pattern that we established years ago. However, no single pattern brings out the best in everyone. We must be adaptable, but first we must be discerning. Sometimes it is necessary to look beyond what initially appears obvious to discover what actually is the case. For example, a young woman in our congregation seemed to like to joke and kid. Because it is easy for me to joke and kid, I responded accordingly. Later I found out that my response annoyed her. She felt that I did not value her.

Some people need a lot of closeness. Others are offended or threatened by closeness. Those who need closeness will best respond to those who can give them a great deal of time. And they expect "quality time." They are eager to socialize, whether at your place or theirs. They want to share deeply from the heart and they expect others to do likewise with them. They *may* like to touch and be touched. They will be quick to extend favors, and equally quick to anticipate them. If they are denied the closeness they consider to be normative, they may become "thorns in the side" of those they feel have rejected them or taken them for granted. All you have to do to get into trouble with some people is nothing.

Those who do not like closeness expect us to be warm and kind but to "keep our distance." If we care to have active, cordial relationships with them, we must allow them to set the limits. They will resent anything they perceive to be invasions of their privacy. Don't ask them how old they are or

70

where they bought that new dress. Just tell them how handsome they are or how beautiful the dress is. Speak to them, but beware of too much touching.

Some people like open dialogue about issues and differences of opinion. Others will "get their feelings hurt" that way. The person who "wants to talk about it," who is eager to "clear the air," will respond best to substantive rather than "polite" conversation. He wants to know where we are coming from and, of course, feels a compulsion to tell us where he is coming from. He will be very uncomfortable with evasiveness or "soft-pedaling" because it indicates to him that we are not taking him or the issue seriously. He will suffer from considerable tension if denied dialogue. Providing we speak civilly and nonjudgmentally, "up-front" people often handle differences of opinion rather well. However, it is crucial to know when a reply is invited and when it is not. Sometimes aggressive persons wish only to be heard. They will be complimented and gratified by a gracious silence. By so honoring them, we may earn the right at a future time to speak plainly in return.

The faint of heart do not appreciate confrontation. If we are too bold or blunt, we will seem unkind, perhaps even unchristian. They will respond better to the soft voice, the subtle comment. They are easily crushed, but will learn to trust those who are consistently gentle.

Some people want to make decisions based on strict logic. Others prefer to react at the "gut level." Those who are deliberate will serve best when provided with the facts, when allowed to weigh all the options, when given time to proceed with caution. They will not appreciate being told to "have faith," or to "trust us," nor can their cooperation be gained by accusing them of being obstructionists or antagonists. To accept them we must accept their thoroughness. On the other hand, those inclined to be spontaneous and visionary need to be encouraged to be patient. They are prone to frustration and an early exit.

Some people are basically angry. Due to unfair treatment

(at least that's how they see it) when they were younger or to present trying circumstances, these people tend to be irritable and short-tempered. If we recognize those who are like this, we will be on the alert rather than being surprised by their actions or reactions. To avoid needlessly arousing such people, we need to be sensitive to their low threshold of tolerance.

Angry people will become only more angry when they encounter argument or criticism. To indulge in either is to "ask for it." Angry people can initiate hostility, so we may be hooked into arguing with them or criticizing them. It takes discipline not to do so. Angry people respond best to patience and kindness. Insight into the reason behind the anger makes it possible to verbalize empathy. Angry people need calm and simplicity. They may respond favorably to humor in the midst of conflict, but they also may be more enraged by it. Those whose anger has a long history will always need to be treated gingerly. Those whose anger is situational will become more congenial as circumstances change.

Some people are filled with anxiety. Anxious people tend to operate the same as angry people. Consequently, the same treatment is appropriate. Tension and resentment set anxious people on edge. Our business is to lead them away from the edge, not to push them over. Lashing back at anxious people is destructive. Reassurance of God's love may be supportive, but glib promises that "everything is going to be just fine" are not helpful. Nor are admonitions such as "calm down!" or "loosen up." Anxious people need to be surrounded by serenity and to be given only maintenance responsibilities.

Some people are afflicted with guilt. The guilt may be expressed as anger, withdrawal, self-condemnation, defensiveness, a critical attitude, or other symptoms. Condemnation and preachments come across to such people as extensions of their own self-accusing finger. On the other hand, to lavishly praise them is not helpful, for it adds to their feelings of unworthiness. To urge that they reject their feelings of guilt will only convince them that we do not understand. The guilt-laden do like to hear that God loves them, and, if they are convinced we are sincere, that we love them. Sometimes our own personal testimonies of forgiveness and deliverance can be meaningful. Guilt-ridden people need gentle encouragement to seek God's forgiveness and to forgive themselves. They need to be treated as forgiven.

Some people are depressed. Depression may be expressed as overindulgence, non-communicativeness, aloofness, docility, unproductivity, threats of self-destruction, or other symptoms. People who are depressed are not helped by criticism. They should not be scolded for being "down in the dumps," even though at times we are inclined to suspect too much self-pity. Neither do they need false or unfounded encouragement. They do need someone who cares, active listening, and simple deeds of kindness.

Some people are suspicious. They will not respond well to being excluded from the decision-making process, to the withholding of information, political maneuverings, to messages with double meanings, to stampede tactics, to head games, or to gestures that seem too good to be true. Try to put one over on a suspicious person and he may oppose everything you do after that. Suspicious people want to be informed. They want procedures prescribed and strictly adhered to, honest answers, detailed explanations, sound defense for policies and actions, and a good amount of input.

Some people are insecure. Insecure people need a lot of support, but not too much. We must know when to let them lean on us and when not to. By allowing too much dependency, we only perpetuate their inability to stand on their own two feet. If we do not allow enough dependency, they will likely feel deserted. If we fail them in either extreme, they will resent us. Insecure people should not be given "big, important jobs" to build up their confidence. If they are not qualified, they will probably fail—thus thinking even less of themselves and resenting us for setting them up to make fools of themselves. Instead, they need to be trusted with small assignments with which they can feel moderately comfortable and have a high probability of success. Obviously, recognition needs to be given when success is achieved. When the insecure person fails he especially needs proof of continued faith in spite of failure.

After having been pastored for a number of years by a man who seemed distant and austere, a change in congregational affiliation brought me into contact with a pastor who was quite the opposite. He was a "people person" who seemed both to draw life from and impart it to members of our little congregation. Despite some major personal shortcomings, his ability to interact positively with all manner of people serves to this day as a model for me. To the angry he brought a pleasant congeniality. To the anxious he brought a casual calm. To the guilt ridden he brought the transparency of his own humanness. To the depressed he brought a contagious light-heartedness. To the suspicious he brought a childlike trust. To the insecure he brought the commitment of his friendship. Every pastor should "go and do likewise."

8
Those Who
Feel Inferior

The beginning of all healthy relationships is proper respect for oneself. The reverse of this follows naturally; a poor attitude toward self will produce tension between self and others. Tragically, many people grow up with keen feelings of inferiority, inadequacy, and unworthiness.

A lot of folks in the family of God feel inferior. They know all about how God loves them. They have been told numerous times how much we love them. Still, they don't feel loved, and they don't act loved. The reason: they don't love themselves. A long time ago they became convinced that they weren't up to par, and to this day they believe it.

Any number of factors may cause feelings of inferiority: being criticized or rejected by one's parents, growing up in poverty, experiencing discrimination, having a physical handicap or disfigurement, family disgrace, unfavorable comparison with a sibling, or an overly protective or domineering parent. Some people can tell you why they feel as they do about themselves. Others cannot. A few don't seem to realize that a problem exists, or they are not aware of its nature.

TRAITS OF INFERIORITY

A person with serious feelings of inferiority may adopt one or more of at least twenty personality traits by which to compensate for inadequacy. These traits are as apt to be disruptive to relationships within the family of God as elsewhere.

1. Selfishness. Attention, service, praise, affection, and possessions are some of the things that, for some people, compensate for a lack of a sense of importance. No one likes being selfish, but inwardly they feel compelled to take and take and take—always under the illusion that being the center of attention proves that they are somebody.

Hilda had a reputation for being selfish. Other men's wives would click their tongues and say, "Poor Gus. Hilda makes him do all the housework; she spends all his money on clothes for herself, and she complains constantly about her health." Now, Hilda was not a bad person. Not really. I rather liked her. It was just that she thought so poorly of herself that she forced Gus to try to convince her otherwise. Of course he was never able to do it. He probably didn't even realize what he was supposed to be doing.

2. Bullheadedness. A person who feels inferior never will be able to admit being wrong or mistaken. To do so would betray a closely guarded secret, namely, that they are not worth much. A person who has no other claim to fame has to hang on to omniscience. Always being right is proof of importance. Harley never lost an argument. He always had a comeback. Neither did he have many friends in the church youth group.

3. Overbearing. Not everyone who thinks poorly of himself shrinks into the corner like a lamb. Some come out like a lion, determined to win friendship or adoration, thus justifying themselves. During Edith's first time at the missionary circle meeting, she so dominated the scene that one would have thought her the senior member. Several of the women "turned her off." They didn't realize she was only saying, "Look at me. I'm important too."

4. Withdrawal. Edith's opposite number is the person with whom you cannot make friends, no matter how hard you try.

This person's attitude is, "Look, you really don't see anything desirable about me. Let's face it, I'm untouchable. Don't tempt me with your insincere friendship. I've been hurt enough already. Go away and let me be lonely in peace."

5. Overmotivation. The person who thinks poorly of himself may seek to compensate by being a success—financially, socially, or professionally. Such people often are quite productive and achieve deserved preeminence in the secular world. However, when their lust for position is manifested in the church, it often precipitates jealousy and strife, even when service is well intended and efficiently rendered.

At the close of a prayer retreat, an elderly woman asked if she might speak to me privately. She confessed that she was fighting a real battle with resentment. It seems that a newcomer had rapidly usurped three of the most prestigious positions in the church, including one of hers. Reportedly this had been the other woman's pattern as she had moved from church to church. This being true, it would be an obvious case of someone trying to substantiate her significance by "showing her stuff." Having done so in any given place, there would be little left for her to do but repeat the act elsewhere. Moving would be an escape from having irritated most of the church in her climb to the top.

6. Undermotivation. Here we have the reverse of the person described above. Underachievers are usually so convinced of their own futility that they simply don't try very hard to succeed. They are commonly thought of as lazy or limited. The truth is that in most instances all they need is a reason to believe in themselves. Gene, a very winsome person, drifted from job to job, with long intervals of unemployment between. Eventually his wife left him because he did not support her. Somewhere back through the years he decided there was no overcoming a minor handicap that held him back, so he quit trying. We can't keep him in church because his failure complex carries over to his religious life.

7. Arrogance. A well-known preacher tells of his surprise when a comment about him came back second-handedly, "He doesn't need anybody." The comment referred to his independent air. But the impression was not an honest one. "The fact is," said the minister, "I have a great need for other people. What others think has always been too important to me." Some people carry their inferiority as superiority. It is a subterfuge. By displaying an attitude just the opposite of the one really felt, they hope to direct attention away from their assumed inferiority. The person who implies he does not need the love of the rest of the church probably is the very one who feels most keenly its absence.

8. Braggadocio. Bragging operates on the same principle of deception as arrogance, only it is expressed in words rather than in bearing. In much boasting, the braggart is only saying, "Since no one has a good word to say for me, I'll say it myself." In doing so, however, he isolates himself, since even in the church people resist the proud.

9. Detachment. Some who feel insignificant do not retreat into a shell. Nor do they bowl people over. Instead, they develop a sophisticated tactic that seeks some middle ground while still preserving the hang-up. Thus they associate freely and even impressively with the group. They are there, and not there. They enter into conversations, but keep the talk trivial. They never reveal hopes or fears, strengths or weaknesses, virtues or vices. They remain something of a mystery even to those who know them best. They are phantoms, if not phonies. Thus, they deprive themselves of that intimate fellowship that makes church affiliation meaningful. They never feel close to anyone. They remain hidden because they feel that if their true selves were ever revealed, they would be rejected.

10. Easily offended. Alice and her husband had drifted from one church to another. She was barren, insecure, and unfulfilled. For the most part she had not related well to her pastors, but when a new minister came to the church, she made a bold and gracious bid for his friendship, and that of his family. For a time, theirs was a model relationship.

However, because he did not comprehend the suspicion and feelings of unworthiness that beset her, the pastor thoughtlessly stepped on the toes of her family's pride. Instantly, she and her household retreated in anger. When the pastor tried to make amends, she was defensive. She said, "We've been through this enough. If we can't get along with you, we'll just quit," and quit they did, rather than risk further hurt.

The person who must be "handled with kid gloves" has a very poor self-image and is consequently offended by any remark or handling that tends to confirm a suspicion of being unwelcome or unappreciated. Sometimes those who feel rejected retaliate. At worst, it may mean an organized offensive to get rid of the pastor. At least, it means chronic criticism of the "in group." An easily offended person will remain basically unhappy until consoled or until time has healed the wounds. For the duration of his anger, nothing about the church will please him (except its failures). He will neither dance when piped to nor mourn when others weep.

11. Jealousy. The person who thinks poorly of himself resents those who excel or who possess what he covets as a means to his own validation. The sight or mention of those who by comparison magnify his shortcomings is like waving a red flag. He will find it easy to speak ill of them, hard not to treat them coolly. Jealousy is a monkey wrench in the fellowship of the church.

12. Overdependency. There are at least two reasons why the person who feels inferior may resort to overdependency: (a) Having no confidence in himself, he is likely to feel helpless, looking to others for direction and assistance. (b) Needing to be the center of attraction, he may find it ego-boosting to have someone else act as his secretary of state. Such people really use their pastor. Pastors who need to be depended upon to bolster their own sense of self-worth respond readily to the overly dependent. They may succeed in carrying such people along, but they never help them become whole persons, and a pastoral change leaves the overly dependent person in a dilemma.

13. Overindependence. This is arrogance put into practice. Not every person who feels inferior confesses it by dependency. Some, instead, try to deny it by ultra-independence. They may help others within the church, but they want no help from anyone. Thus, in their own way they rob themselves of real fellowship, just as do the detached. The way to meaningful relationships in the church (as well as without) is neither through dependence nor independence, but through *interdependence*. This means both giving and accepting help as occasions make each appropriate.

14. Gossip. We talk about people for one of two reasons: (a) by spreading derogatory information about them, gossips hope to prove them as inferior as they feel, or (b) they hope to gain a friendship or two by being a ready source of news. Whichever the objective, gossip is out of order. People would not resort to such despicable tactics if they thought more highly of themselves.

One day several women of our church were making candy in a room adjacent to our church office. Their chatter could be clearly distinguished from where the secretary sat at her desk. The secretary, who is not a member of our congregation, observed something commendable about the conversation going on outside her door. She said, "They don't gossip." Hour after hour these women worked, talking constantly, but not once did any of them feel it necessary to court attention by gossiping.

15. Possessiveness. Inferiority is equated with being unlovable. Then can you imagine what it means to a person who feels inferior to find someone who genuinely does seem to love him? This love must be guarded. It must be squeezed tight, lest it get away. It must have constant confirmation. Its staying power must repeatedly be questioned. It will find rejection without cause. The person who feels inferior may, in his possessiveness, alienate himself from the few friends he has enjoyed in the church. This only adds to the sense of isolation and intensifies feelings of resentment and frustration.

16. Tightwad. "Since no one thinks well of me, I must look out for myself." So reasons an occasional person who lacks self-love. Not having a sense of belonging creates great insecurity, for it is in community that we survive. Most, if not all, of the people in the church who are poor stewards suffer from feelings of inferiority, manifested as either selfishness or insecurity. They ask no quarter and give none. The reason: they are convinced it would do no good.

17. Do-gooding. The do-gooder feels quite the opposite of the tightwad. The do-gooder still has a few hopes. He believes it just may be possible to *earn* (dare I say, buy) a few friends by generosity. Certainly this is not to say that all who are generous and helpful are neurotic. I am only pointing out that one of the ways by which some people hope to compensate for their inferiority is by making the church, as a whole or a few members, obligated to them. Elmira worked diligently for the church. When she wasn't adequately praised, she left, saying, "No one appreciated me."

81

18. Vanity. One need not be a wicked witch to feel a compulsion to be the fairest of them all. All he or she may need is the impression that physical attractiveness is the key to popularity. The charge that some people go to church to show off their clothes is not without foundation. But it isn't a healthy church if the object every Sunday seems to be to outdress the rest of the congregation. A beautiful spirit is more to be desired than fine clothes, yea much more than fancy wardrobes.

19. Lust. Lust is tragic in any fellowship. It is most unfortunate within the congregation of the righteous. Yet, occasionally there comes to the church circle one so destitute of love as to seek it at any level and at any price. Because love is more freely given within the fellowship of the church, it is only natural that those longing for it should seek it there. They become a problem, however, when they transgress moral boundaries. Moral laxity is a sign of desperation, a cue to the cheapness with which one views himself.

A fifteen-year-old girl, active in the church yet promiscuous, confessed to her pastor during a counseling session, "I have always felt so insignificant." Apparently feeling rejected by her mother, she gave herself to this boy and that one, looking for an acceptance she could not find.

20. Perfectionism. Perfectionism usually is admired, as well it might be. Yet slavish perfectionism indicates feelings of inferiority. Through perfection, the person who lacks self-acceptance hopes to attain a level of performance worthy of acceptance. Paul tried that as a Pharisee. The impossible demands of the law nearly drove him to insanity. Then he learned about grace. Thereafter, he said, "Not as though I had already attained, either were already perfect: but I follow after" (Phil. 3:12 KJV).

The perfectionist will not have many friends, even in the church. He will be uncomfortable around others, and will make them uncomfortable around him. The perfectionist is always "up-tight" lest something embarrass him (that something being anything that would reveal his finitude). His preciseness harasses people. They feel they must be perfect around him. Think what this does to the perfectionist's children! They can't relax, be comfortable, or even human.

Ruby was a perfectionist. Her house was always immaculate. She was always perfectly groomed. Her family was always alerted to be on their toes to act properly. She was in many ways an unselfish, admirable person. Still when she headed up a department in the church work there was constant controversy. Because she could not tolerate failure in herself, she pushed everyone else too hard.

A person who finds himself repeatedly resentful and

82

creating resentment should look inwardly, not outwardly for the cause. The chances are good that the cause is rooted in feelings of inferiority. An examination of his behavior pattern is likely to reveal one or more of the traits covered in this chapter. A professing Christian has no recourse but to confess his faults (yes, sin) and to seek healing through repentance, counseling, and other necessary means.

Recently, one of our most respected members told how for years he had suffered repeatedly from hurt feelings, and had responded in petty ways to inadvertent injustices. Now he knows why that had been his practice. He still is sensitive (both God and the rest of us can forgive him for that), but he identifies the blame as his own. He has learned to act responsibly. As such he helps all of us to "keep the unity of the Spirit in the bond of peace."

9
Those Who
Resent Authority

No single personality type poses more of a hazard to the harmony of a local congregation than does the person who is hostile toward authority figures. Because of an obsessive fear of domination, this person will be threatened by the pastor's power at the slightest provocation. Because of a compulsion to demonstrate that he or she is no longer dominated (as in childhood), the individual hostile toward authority may from time to time test and even challenge the position of the pastor.

A person who is allergic to power in others is usually very strong. Over the years that person has developed a life-style in which force meets force.

The individual who is hostile toward authority is, in fact, a frustrated monarch. Were it possible, that person would become a supreme ruler, and thus, with absolute authority, eliminate all other sources of power and be forever free of the fear of domination by others. This, of course, is the height of folly. Herod and Caesar are classic examples of those who have succeeded in gaining a monopoly on power and are plagued by the fear of being deposed.

There is a god-almightiness about those hostile to authority. It must come to that, since even God, the ultimate authority, has to be equaled or surpassed to put all authority beneath rather than above such people.

Such persons are commonly referred to as the "church

boss." There still are bosses, particularly among smaller churches (that's the primary reason they are still small). Mark it down: the church boss is hostile toward authority. That's how he got his office. He is the resident demagogue. The pastor may be a demagogue, too. However, he is the guest demagogue. If the two take up arms against each other, one will become demagogue emeritus.

During the era when the pattern of the local church called for the pastor to be a paternal figure, dominant in authority with few boards and councils to which he was accountable, the church boss was almost a necessary evil. The pastor's raw authority brought the blood rushing to the brain of the person hostile to authority. Either self-appointed or chosen by consensus from among other less brave dissidents, he was to be the fire in the pew to fight the fire in the pulpit.

With the coming of more representative church government, the would-be church boss may now lack a cause. While deprived of the fulfillment of a knock-down-drag-out battle with the pastor (which had great therapeutic value as an outlet for hostilities), the church boss is placated by not being so often threatened now by the prospect of domination. Of course those annoyed by authority figures can have trouble with other members of the congregation (particularly those of their own stripe) as well as with the pastor.

It is not hard to identify people who are hostile toward authority. They thrive on arguments and are authorities on almost everything. If you say, "It is a nice day," they say, "Looks like rain." If offered a favor, they will decline, no matter how badly they need it. They—this is a dead giveaway—order their children around as if they are drill sergeants and their children are new recruits.

The points at which the pastor and people hostile toward authority come to confrontation are numerous. To begin with, people who dislike authority figures will bristle at strong preaching with which they disagree. Even if they do not know the speaker, each one will peg him, usually subconsciously, as "just like my old man." Whether or not the preacher is aware of their presence in the congregation, the authority rejecters are apt to feel that they are the direct object of each sermon. To them, every loud voice is intimidating because it brings back memories of childhood and home.

It may be helpful to understand the background of those who resist authority. Many grew up in an era of totalitarianism. Authority was wielded with little restraint both in the work place and in the home. Many people were raised in families where the father was a dominant, perhaps brutal, force to be reckoned with constantly. If the father did not "rule the roost," mother did. The person, fifty years of age or older, who has spent the past thirty years or more being defensive toward those in positions of authority is almost common. Typically such an individual was victimized by dictatorial parents who denied their child self-expression and normal independence. Legions of these left the church about the time they graduated from high school, entered military service or college, or married.

Many who remain in the church are pillars. They hold offices, perform many essential (and not so essential) tasks, and give money. Most congregations would not know what to do without them. Pastors, sometimes, don't know what to do with them. Some who resent authority are relatively covert in their resistance. Instead of organizing a fight against the pastor, they simply function as roadblocks to progress whenever they feel themselves pressured. They express doubts, vote no, and otherwise grouse about unrelated matters.

It is not uncommon for those who resent authority to have hate/love feelings toward authority figures. While they are angered by attempts at directing them and compelled to resist such attempts, on the other hand, they may feel some need for direction and admire those strong enough to give it. Such, of course, were the feelings they developed toward their parents. When confronted with power, they were always torn between obeisance and rebellion. They still are. Whether a person passively resists authority or is ambivalent in his reaction to it, he is likely to confuse the pastor by the obscure or contradictory signals he sends forth.

Those in the family of God who have a problem with authority are not limited to the middle-aged and older crowd. To their number must be added some products of the sixties and seventies. Raised by permissive parents, they despise rules and rule makers. Sensitized by the war in Vietnam and Watergate, they carry resentment toward almost all social structures. Often articulate, extremely idealistic, and college educated, this new generation has its own reasons for resisting authority. The situation is especially volatile when extreme idealism encounters a firm pragmatism in the pastor. Neither is likely to understand the other's position, nor to make allowance for it. Unlike their older counterparts who are institutionally oriented, this generation is generally anti-institutional. Many have found the traditional forms and beliefs of the church intolerable, but some are still trying to make a go of it in the church, either because of allegiance to it or genuine devotion to Jesus Christ (or both).

No matter which generation they represent or the degree of their resistance, those who are hostile to authority cannot be ignored. Their opposition may be too formidable, and their cooperation is too valuable. Ways must be found to work with them and to maximize their contributions. In order to do this, the pastor must watch his style as well as his methods. Those who resent authority are alarmed by a pompous demeanor and by pulpit-pounding demands. They generally expect the pastor to speak softly and *not* to carry a big stick. Those who are institutionally oriented may like opinionated statements, which support their own biases, but will take exception to any emphasis that is contrary to their views.

Those hostile toward authority cannot be rushed. Their trust must be painstakingly cultivated. It is crucial to involve them in the democratic process. Their toughness can be a great asset. They make great partners, but they must be treated like partners, not pawns.

Whereas the person who suffers from an inferiority

complex will take it hard if he loses an election, the person who suffers from an authority figure complex will take it hard if he loses an issue. The former will need to win at the polls to reassure him of his acceptance. The latter will need to win at the conference table to reassure him of his independence. One says to the pastoral leadership of the congregation, "Don't pass me by." The other says, "Don't push me."

Those who are hostile toward authority *may* be a problem in the family of God. Those who have a compulsion to control are almost *certain* to be a problem. Since a power struggle with them is nearly inescapable (short of flight or capitulation), they are likely to divide the church. These people will deny the pastor the authority he needs to lead the congregation. They will deny other members of the congregation opportunity to share in philosophic or policy-making decisions.

Aaron was such a person. Capable of great charm, witty, competent in some areas, and admirably dedicated, he had over the years been involved in several devastating schisms within the congregation. When not aroused by the pastor's leadership, he could be magnanimous and complimentary. However, whenever it appeared that the church was going forward without his approval, he would arch his back and do about whatever it took to defeat the pastor. More than a few people had great confidence in Aaron and could be counted on to side with him in any dispute that might arise. Others resented him and held him responsible for dividing the church or hindering its progress.

Not all of the Aarons in the church sit on the board of trustees. Some are quite content to allow others to hold the official positions and to do the routine work of the church. However, if a fundamental issue arises or a crucial decision is to be made, they let it be known how things are to go. Those who hold the official positions have been chosen as "stand-ins" or are so intimidated by the boss that, even against their wills, they yield to pressure. Pastors come and go, but laypersons live in the community and must "get along" with

89

one another. Every congregation has an informal power structure as well as a formal one. The shakers and movers not included in the formal power structure must still be taken into consideration in the governance of the church.

The church boss who is content to maintain a low profile so long as no major issues or decisions are before the congregation is not likely to oppose the pastor, providing he sticks to preaching the Word, visiting the sick, and running the mimeograph machine. In other words, if the pastor is a hard-working, faithful employee with no managerial aspirations, his position is quite secure. Church bosses who want to tell him how to spend his time and money, what to preach, and what to wear, are the most intolerable of all.

When coping with people who must control, it is important to discover what is behind that compulsion. It may be that they, like hostile people, resent authority. Their aggression against authority figures is greater, however.

No matter for what reason a prominent or not so prominent member feels compelled to exercise control, it is basic to win their friendship so that both they and the pastor will value their relationship. Special effort can be made to invite their input and to test the acceptability of plans. Continuing, sometimes candid, dialogue is imperative. It is advisable to bring other strong persons to surrounding positions of leadership, thus making it difficult for any single person to dominate. Ultimately, other members of the family of God must share the responsibility for curbing the control of the church boss. The pastor cannot do this single-handedly. He should not attempt to, and he should not be expected to. Loving confrontation by peers will best convince the boss to relinquish control to others, including the pastor. Although the pastor must never pit loyal laypersons against the church boss, he can invite responsible leadership from the elected officers of the church. Subsequently, they must feel the pastor's gentle support for them and his redemptive spirit toward the church boss.

In unavoidable confrontations with the church boss,

win/win solutions should be sought. Win/lose solutions are costly. Family ties are of more value than partisan positions. The worth of all persons must be affirmed above all problems that exist.

When a bitter dispute arose between the herdsmen of Abraham's cattle and those of Lot, Abraham said to his nephew, "Let there be no strife between you and me, and between your herdsmen and my herdsmen; for we are kinsmen" (Gen. 13:8). Even though Abraham and Lot separated, each maintained dignity and goodwill toward the other. Later, Abraham risked his life to rescue Lot from wicked captors.

Remember, even when we disagree, we are kinfolk; we are family.

It is not wise to openly disagree with the person who feels hostile toward authority figures. What sounds like constructive criticism to others sounds to him like a reprimand. What sounds to others like a mild request sounds to him like a demanding order. When speaking to or even in the presence of such a person, strong, opinionated statements should be avoided. They remind him of the person(s) responsible for his hang-up.

It is best to ask the advice of those who feel hostile toward authority, rather than displaying too much initiative. Such persons welcome inclusion on the leadership team, often accept and discharge responsibility very well, and are unusually loyal to the person who, by a democratic approach, bestows the equality of which they have often felt deprived.

As the pastor considers the variety of persons in the congregation, he will discover two reasons for wanting all of them to be happy. One is the shepherd's noble desire to care for his flock. The other is purely selfish: unhappy people sow unhappiness wherever they go—including in the church—and that adds to a pastor's job. Whether people are unhappy because of maladjustment or because of a crisis that has temporarily made life miserable, they are not often easy to cope with, and woe unto the lamb who must feed beside them.

A church fellowship of any size will include a few who suffer from emotional complications. Does this mean conflict is unavoidable? Definitely not. A congregation can maintain balance despite the presence of disturbed persons. Indeed the church must not only accept such persons, but actually be involved in their therapy. A local congregation can absorb a rather large number of distraught members, provided pastoral care and the maturity of fellow members are adequate. Otherwise, however, one or two offenders may spark a conflagration that will spread throughout the fellowship.

As the church sails into the angry waters of interpersonal stress, the pastor is the prow. He must lead the way and meet the waves in such a way that it makes smooth, rather than turbulent, sailing. Here he will need a great share of the grace of God within his own soul. If he doesn't love people and sincerely want to help them, if he doesn't believe, as Jesus did that the sick have need of a physician, he is in the wrong profession. Inevitably, he will be part of the problem instead of part of the solution.

A pastor must pray without ceasing to have compassion, not only for the multitude, but for that lonely figure who trudges to his study, or the one who cries out to him from behind the crowd, or the one who simply looks at him longingly. Most of all, he should pray to have compassion for the one who despitefully uses him. This one, beyond all others, is sending out S.O.S. signals.

However, the pastor will need more than love. He must also have wisdom and knowledge in order to facilitate the healing of distressed and distressing members of his congregation. He is responsible, insofar as is humanly possible, to see that those unhappy people dotting the pews find happiness before they bring unhappiness to the entire congregation and/or great damage to themselves. His ministry, then, becomes, in effect, the salvation of his ministry. By restoring individuals, he preserves the group.

The pastor's training should have equipped him for the task. Given sufficient psychological insight his administration of the church and informal contacts with members of the congregation will take into consideration sore spots identified by experience. This will keep him out of a lot of trouble, and very legitimately win him much favor among those gratified by his warm friendship, a welcome contrast to the many unhappy associations they have experienced.

Not only will the pastor need to analyze personality idiosyncrasies, he will teach his people to identify them in themselves and in others, in each instance making allowance for them. In this way he generates forbearing attitudes. Usually he will not do this directly, such as saying, "Tom, you must overlook George's actions because he never resolved his Oedipus complex," but in a nonpersonal way point out why we all suffer from unwelcome feelings.

A congregation educated in the ways of the human personality is able to live more peaceably with itself. Members not only understand their own peculiarities, they understand those of their brethren. They control their own behavior with greater efficiency, and forgive the errant behavior of others with greater ease.

Often the pastor's ministry to the troubled personality includes formal counseling. (In difficult cases referral to a counselor with more advanced skills is recommended.) Usually, members seek their pastor, but sometimes he must take the initiative. In the privacy of his study, pastor and layperson can explore together the source of inner unrest. Fears, resentments, complexes, and doubts can be aired. An explanation for each is sought and frequently found. Armed with creative insights, the counselee is ready to conquer troublesome hang-ups. And often, with God's help, there is success.

One by one, marriages are saved, parent-child relationships are improved, bitterness between in-laws is resolved, misunderstandings within the congregation are healed, and people begin to live the abundant life. Wherever you find these miracles taking place, there you will find an understanding church.

10
Young and Old: Members with Unique Needs

While conducting a conference at a local congregation, I was approached by two long-standing members who were concerned that their church seemed to be dying. Although they did not hold the pastor solely responsible for this situation, these two laypersons were critical of their pastor's performance. Specifically, they charged, "The young people just can't relate to him at all." The pastor, however, enjoyed excellent rapport with older members of the congregation.

What this suggests is that each generation in any congregation has its own expectations of the pastor. Points of identification with him will vary widely. He, in turn, will find it much easier to relate to some age groups than to others. Yet, he is called to be the pastor of everyone from the smallest child to the oldest adult. He will need to understand the needs of every generation represented in the church.

The generation gap is not a figment of some psychologist's imagination. It is very real. Furthermore, it exists between *all* generations. Each generation is at a different stage of development and consequently finds it difficult to relate to older and younger generations. Our needs, desires, values, tastes, philosophies, and hang-ups are conditioned by age. Both past experiences and present struggles set each generation apart from every other one. We need to accept, rather than judge, those of different generations than our own.

Although we may be able to narrow it, we cannot close the generation gap. I doubt the wisdom of doing so even if we could. We detect the ingenious workings of God here. Each generation has its own special contribution to make to society in general and to the family of God in particular. For the good of the whole of mankind generational distinctives should survive. Moreover, the generations need to live together harmoniously, without insisting on conformity from one another. "Learning to love" someone twenty-five years older or younger than ourselves can be a delightful challenge. It can also broaden our horizons.

The church must carefully strategize how to bridge generation gaps. Although inter-generational experiences are desirable, it is also important to acquaint each generation with its own uniqueness and to encourage appreciation for those distinctives. If members of any generation comprehend why they think and behave as they do, that is a beginning. If they come to know why those of other generations think and behave as they do, that is a major breakthrough. The local church needs not only to promote inter-generational under-standings but also to accommodate all generations. Contented people tend to be less critical of one another.

Generation gaps inevitably have great ramifications within the church where members of the family of God of all ages share in worship, ministry, fellowship, and witness. Approaches to each of these activities may vary greatly from the young to the old. Furthermore, the generations may not agree on beliefs and are almost certain to disagree on life-styles. Acceptable conduct may be hotly debated, just as it is in many households. Does all of this add up to a mission impossible? No, not necessarily.

Let us consider the age groupings normally present in a local congregation, with special attention to their respective characteristics and needs. Not every member of any given generation will necessarily fit the profile given here, but generally speaking, similarities among persons of the same generation are a valuable guide when working with diverse groups of people.

96

YOUTH

It is essential to assess the needs of young people and to provide programming accordingly. Youth is an age marked by the following struggles—

1. The struggle for recognition. Youth are attempting to "crash" the adult world. Like minority groups they are seeking equality, an equality that, of necessity, has been denied them during the years of childhood. Equality is conditioned upon mutual respect. Thus young people want to be heard. They do not feel heard when they are put down or ignored. Longing for a place in the adult community, they timidly or brashly put forth overtures that may be accepted or rejected. It is crucial to their spiritual and social development that they be *accepted.*

If such overtures are graciously received—even when they leave something to be desired—the young person moves forward with increased confidence and productivity, concluding, "The church is fair and open-minded. There is a place for me. I am valued as a person."

However, a young person whose overtures are spurned may retreat into isolation from the church or become a highly vocal critic of the church. In either case the capacity to adapt to the church and the potential for being fully assimilated into the church will be impaired, perhaps for life.

The church that desires to conserve its young people will utilize them in worship and in mission activities. Moreover, room will be made for young people in the leadership and decision-making processes of the church.

2. The struggle for independence. Erickson describes adolescence as the period of search for identity. Every youth strives to become an entity in his own right. He feels he must break away from parental domination, and perhaps the domination of society in general or certain institutions in particular (including the church). Imposed subjection thwarts him in his attempt to stamp himself as an individual. Consequently, the

97

church may alienate some young people if it insists on conformity to prescribed standards. They may resist, not only because the standards are too strict, but because they represent the thinking of the older generation and, hence, represent a threat to the youth's own identity.

Much of the motivation behind extreme forms of dress and grooming is an aggravated attempt to establish (or preserve) a sense of selfhood. Allowed more individuality within the church, youth would not have to make such emphatic statements about who they are or what they stand for. Nor would they have to go outside the church for acceptance. It is imperative that young people be permitted to present their youthfulness with dignity and pride. Thus they should be encouraged to express their tastes and viewpoints so as not to feel defensive about either.

3. The struggle for gratifying experiences. Toy cars and dolls no longer suffice. Youth are looking for satisfactions that elude them. They desperately pursue bold new thrills. Puberty and wider exposure to the world vastly increase physical and emotional appetites and capabilities. Intellectual capabilities also increase, adding the need for intellectual stimulation. Youth may want to experience more and do more than is sometimes advisable. Here the church often appears as a big spoil-sport. At the same time when youth feel driven to experiment, the church always seems to be exclaiming, "No! No!"

Without denying youth's desire for independence and adventure, the church must help its young people constructively address the pressure to engage in sex, drugs, alcohol, and other destructive activities. To minimize conflict with youthful drives, the church needs to give early attention to education, focusing on moral principles and Christian values long before popular practices become a battleground between the generations. The church will also be wise to work closely with the home in instilling a love for virtue and decency. Internal restraints ultimately prove far more effective than external ones.

4. The struggle for meaning. Youth are searching for foundations, something they can believe with certainty. They should find it, of all places, in the church.

Young people can be deceived, and therefore may be gullible about what the church teaches as well as about what others teach. However, the church must never presume upon the naïveté of young people. The message of the Christian faith must be presented with integrity. I have sometimes blushed over the answers given to bright young students by their parents, Sunday school teachers, and pastors. Glib, simplistic, and downright nonsensical replies or pronouncements only diminish their respect for the church. Young people can usually accept it that faith transcends reason, but why should they accept illogical answers that insult their own intelligence? If the church is to speak with authority, its answers must be on a high scholastic level.

The Christian faith needs to be presented to young people so as to make it relevant to their temptations, accountable to their questions, reassuring to their fears, strengthening to their character, and insightful to their concerns. Each of us identifies only with what touches our own life. Young people are attracted to the church that leads them to experience God as a real and loving Presence, gives authentic reasons for choosing good over evil, channels their altruistic ambitions into meaningful service, affords genuine hope, and dignifies the existence of mankind.

In the family of God young people should always have reason to thank God that an honest attempt has been made to understand them and to meet their needs.

YOUNG ADULTS

Young adults are frequently the most mobile members of our society. They are also most open to new affiliations, new lifestyles, and new beliefs. That adds up to a great opportunity for the church to reach young adults. It likewise means that the church may easily lose the young adults it takes for granted. Young adults who have experienced the church positively as youth are more inclined to remain with the church than those who have not. Yet the loyalty of neither group is guaranteed. Young adulthood is an age marked by these periods—

1. A time of freedom. Young adults usually are just beginning life on their own. They are free to sleep in on Sunday morning or to take a weekend holiday. No longer can the church rely on mom and dad to get them to worship so it must become more solicitous and enticing. An additional, howbeit unwelcome, byproduct of freedom is that old associations are broken or interrupted. College enrollment, military induction, new vocational pursuits, and wedding bells do have a way of "breaking up that old gang of mine." The single young adult may find it difficult to find a support group in the church. The newly married couple needs to find new ways to relate to the church.

To counteract this disconjunctiveness the church must create a feeling of togetherness through whatever realignments may be called for. Fellowship, service, and specialized programs are all crucial in ministering to young adults.

100

2. A time of adjustment. Monumental changes face every person making the transition from youth to adulthood. These changes are primarily social and vocational and are usually most pronounced for those who marry. The young couple faces the task of adjusting to one another and to their new roles as husband and wife. Later, they are likely to have to adjust to children and their roles as parents. If the pastor performed their wedding ceremony and has a close relationship with them, he will have counseled them about potential problem areas. When difficulties arise, the couple should feel free to discuss them with their pastor. The church will also need to be supportive and close at hand.

3. A time of heavy responsibility. The young couple starting from scratch faces a long, uphill struggle to become established financially. Income is usually stretched to the limit. The husband may work long hours, or study evenings. The wife is also likely to work. They will find it very convenient to say they have no time for the church. First things may not come first while they rethink values and establish priorities. The young couple may also be embarrassed about their steward-ship obligations. Feeling the financial press, they may resent the church for asking for its portion or feel guilty about being unable to give their fair share.

Still, all young adults have certain abilities that the church must enlist, in order to implement its ministry and to preserve the Christian experience of its members. The church needs discernment in what it asks of young adults, being careful not to ask too much or too little, and to ask for the right things.

Congregations ministering effectively to young adults are typically progressive in both thought and mission. However, congregations dominated by young couples sometimes experi-ence a higher-than-average degree of internal conflict. Imma-turity and the tendency to become chummy make young adults prone to misunderstandings that may fracture relation-ships and disrupt the unity of the church. This is especially true if the pastor and spouse are young adults and allow themselves to be drawn into a clique.

Among the brightest stars in the early church was a young adult, Timothy. His mentor, Paul, helped forge Timo-thy's ministry. Paul's admonition to Timothy was, "Let no one despise your youth" (1 Tim. 4:12). With good mentoring that need never happen to any youth or young adult.

MIDDLE-AGED ADULTS

"As go the middle-aged, so goes the church." In most congregations that axiom would seem to apply. The reasons for this are two: (1) The middle-aged often constitute the largest age group in the church. (2) The church typically depends on the middle-aged for the bulk of its leadership and financial support, since they are usually at the peak of their productivity. Middle age is a time of conservation.

1. The middle-aged are anxious to conserve their investments. They have spent their youth getting what they now have. Some will settle for that. Others are reaching out for still more while clinging to what is already in hand. Whether highly motivated or not, many middle-aged persons have enough to be at least comfortable. Most recognize the inevitable: not all their dreams will come true. There is less urgency to survive. There is less hope, less imagination, and less physical ambition. There is more security, less opportunity.

2. The middle-aged are intent on conserving their identity. Thus, they generally are not inclined toward flexibility. Having identified with the world the way it is (the world with which they grew up and helped to shape), change makes them feel like outsiders, strangers in the *now*. Destroy the status quo and you destroy something of them. The middle-aged are the personification of the status quo. Change forces adjustment. Adjustment is normal for youth, but abnormal for middle age. That's why middle age has been called the period when the broad mind and the narrow waist change places.

102

3. The middle-aged desire to conserve time. They may be avid devotees of the news—listening to it twice, three times, four times each day, perhaps unable to retire at night until after the late news and beginning the new day with the early morning news. Their great interest in the news is attributable to two things: (1) They are concerned with how fast the world (their world) is eroding, that is, to what extent their values and investments are being threatened. (2) In the temporality of events, they are painfully reminded of their own fleeting appearance on the stage of life.

The middle-aged often have an obsession with the present. They reminisce about the past, but they would not want to go back there. They plan for the future but they don't want to get there. No matter where their talk is their hearts are in the present. Why? Because the middle-aged have suddenly realized that they are creatures of time, and time is ticking away! With the passing of youth and the ever-nearing prospect of old age the middle-aged come face to face with their own mortality. Those who are well-adjusted will not spend their time worrying about growing old, but they will find themselves thinking about it.

What does this period of conservatism mean to the church in its ministry to the middle-aged? On the positive side it means that the backbone of the church will come from this age group. Just as other institutions and enterprises count heavily on the middle-aged, so also may the church. Ordinarily they are experienced, qualified, loyal, dependable, and hard-working. Often they are unselfish to a fault and allow themselves to be used. They require a minimum amount of care. If life is fulfilling to them, they are generally congenial and cooperative.

On the negative side, because of their conservatism, the middle-aged may impede the progress of the church. In their suspicion about change they are apt to discard some good ideas. Furthermore, because they have been around awhile and learned things the hard way, the middle-aged can be smug and give the appearance of being know-it-alls.

Young ministers who leave the church and rail out against its rigidity are usually frustrated with the middle-aged. The middle-aged quite naturally feel the church should be managed as they manage their own lives. That means don't risk much indebtedness; don't be too visionary in your goals; don't mess around with value systems. Of course, not all middle-aged persons take this stance. Those who remain youthful in their outlook provide the church with the best of two worlds. They stand at the forefront of virtually all constructive programs of the church.

Effective ministry to the middle-aged will stimulate their thinking and keep them involved in the changing world around them—including that within the church. Those who resist change should never be isolated as a "thorn in the side" of the

103

pastor or other leaders. While the middle-aged are reminded by the calendar of their mortality, let the church remind them of their immortality as sons and daughters of God. While they accept their disappointments (disappointment has been called a middle age disease), let the church celebrate their accomplishments. While they develop attachments to their secular possessions, let the church raise their sights to "things that are above."

The church given to fads and continually championing change for the sake of change will disrupt the equilibrium of its middle-aged constituents and rob them of the stability they crave. On the other hand, the narrow, reactionary church will also do them great harm by entrenching their alienation from a changing world.

The church and the middle-aged need each other. Each is profoundly affected by the other. If the church can save the middle-aged from despair, negativism, lethargy, and boredom, it will have served them well. They, in turn, will serve it well.

OLDER ADULTS

Old age has been termed a time of simplification. Life becomes less complex for those living in the sunset of life. Many struggles are now behind them. They need less money, fewer activities, and not quite so much company. They have fewer unanswered questions, unresolved conflicts, or burning ambitions. They don't need as much, but what they do need they need very much. The church figures largely in the meeting of those needs, or at least it should. What are those needs?

1. A sense of serenity. If a person's beliefs have been authentic throughout his earlier years, they will be of inestimable value to him when he is old. Knowing what he believes will fortify him against the threats of illness, loneliness, and even death. His attitudinal values will support him when everything else is giving way.

The church needs to reinforce the faith of the elderly. To debunk that faith, even when it seems childlike or quaint, is to strike at the one security the elderly have. When the elderly talk about what their faith means to them, it is not so much whistling in the dark as it is a necessary affirmation of their convictions. In a way they are preaching to themselves in order to strengthen themselves. It is crucial to listen to them supportively.

2. A sense of significance. Let us note again that one's sense of significance derives largely from (a) acceptance, (b) achievement, and (c) autonomy. From the moment of retirement the elderly tend to lose their sense of achievement. This is particularly true for those who strongly identified with their work, especially if their work was an expression of themselves. Moreover, as the elderly become more infirmed, they lose autonomy. They become more dependent upon others, less and less able to care for themselves. Worst of all, the elderly often outlive their peers, thus being deprived of those from whom they experienced much of their acceptance. As they become less active, less alert, less attractive, even family members may shun them, further adding to their loss of acceptance.

What can the church do? It can intentionally address the three A's. The talents of the elderly should be employed, not only to support their sense of achievement but for the good of the church. The elderly are also a source of wisdom and faith. Their counsel can be sought to good advantage, whether formally or informally. Their prayers can be solicited. Even shut-ins may find it possible to perform certain ministries.

While there is little the church can do to preserve the autonomy of the elderly, it can be of great support to them in the loss of their autonomy. Transition times are especially critical. I have watched numerous older persons leave their homes to be transferred to health care facilities—an extremely painful move. Those who face four strange walls with fear, anger, depression, and rapidly failing health need comfort. What a time for ministry!

105

Certainly the church can provide large quantities of acceptance for those who have anemic social calendars. Regular visitation is important. Remembrances on birthdays and other occasions will mean much. One church provides absentee ballots for members who were once active but who no longer can attend the business meetings of the congregation. Elderly people sometimes are self-pitying and complain that the church is not what it used to be because they feel the church has forgotten them. It is no longer "my church," but "their church." This need not be the case.

3. A sense of being cared for. While they do not like to be reminded of it or to have it overly compensated for, the elderly have a variety of needs that create dependence on others. They often need continuing medical care. They must see doctors periodically. They may take several drugs daily. They may need legal advice, or at least help with such items as taxes, insurance, and checking accounts. Their property may need repair. Children do not always provide assistance. The church needs to stay close, and be alert to unmet needs. One congregation had a task force that ran errands and provided services for the elderly and other needy persons. This too is ministry.

106

Between 1970 and 1980, the fastest-growing segment of the U.S. population was people eighty-five years of age and above. In 1900, 3 million in our country were sixty-five years of age or older, representing four percent of the total U.S. population. In 1980, 25.5 million people were sixty-five or above, representing eleven percent of our population. Projections are that by 1990, 28.9 million will have reached or surpassed the age of sixty-five. By the year 2000, that number should reach 30.6 million; and by 2030, it is expected to swell to 51.6 million. At some point the percentage of Americans sixty-five or above will reach thirty percent of the total U.S. population.

Obviously these statistics have profound implications for the church. The church will increasingly be populated by older persons. One mainline denomination already reports that in fifty percent of its congregations the majority of the members have reached or surpassed the age of sixty-five. America is growing older, and so are our congregations!

With the aging of church members comes a responsibility to plan ministries specifically for them. In the past most specialized attention was directed to young people. Many churches employed staff persons to be ministers of youth. In the future the church will find it appropriate to direct much of its attention toward the elderly.

Not only are most Americans living longer; they are living better. Older Americans as a whole have better health, more wealth, more free time, more energy, and more of everything to offer than at any time in our history.

The elderly are coming. Each of us is likely to one day be numbered in their army. They are well worth knowing, loving, and serving. In a congregation I once served the older members call themselves The Invincibles. They are part of a Sunday school class established half a century ago by a woman who was a visionary and premier Christian educator. Her picture still hangs on the wall of their classroom.

These invincibles, some of the most beautiful people I have ever known, remain my good friends. A few years ago class members published their autobiographies in a modest volume compiled by a member. It is a treasure piece, filled with accounts of exciting pilgrimages and vibrant testimonies. Over many decades these great souls have poured their lives into the church. We are their debtors. Our ministry to them is more than an obligation. It is a sincere ''Thank you for a job well done!''

11
The Family
at Worship

Christianity has been described as a religion of ecstasy. Why not, when it is based on faith in a risen Lord? Yet, the fact is that many worshipers on Sunday morning do not experience the kind of ecstasy reported by a newcomer to our church who wrote, ". . .after the great Sunday school lesson and church services Sunday (including your sermon) I wanted to jump into the isle [sic] and click my heals." This man and his wife had been experiencing many trials. He came to church hungry to worship.

Instead, some people experience boredom, or perhaps even guilt or depression during Sunday worship services. One woman said to me, "I always feel so unfulfilled." We go to church hoping to feel, "This is like heaven to me," but sometimes we come away feeling like, "Day is dying in the west."

Mark 2 describes for us what might be considered a model worship service. Certainly the ecstasy was there. Surprisingly not many of us see this experience of extraordinary inspiration as an example of how we might enjoy such blessedness more often than we do. Perhaps we view it as a one-time-only event. But does it really have to be that?

Even a casual reading of the account immediately informs us that few of the traditional worship elements were included in the event. There was no choir anthem, no liturgy,

no pastoral prayer as we know it, and—most unusual of all—
no offering.

This exciting worship service did not take place in an
imposing cathedral, but in a humble home in Capernaum.
There was an overflow crowd, with not so much as standing
room remaining. I am not suggesting that we should do away
with accustomed elements of worship or that we vacate our
church buildings (though on occasion this might prove
beneficial). I am proposing that no matter what else we do or
do not do, we give primary attention to the ingredients for
making worship the vital experience it was that day Jesus
came to Capernaum.

The proclamation of the gospel is central to worship. In
most of our churches the Bible is seen on the communion
table or the pulpit and it is read during the order of worship.
But is it *preached* during the sermon? Token attention to the
Word of God, whether in worship or in preaching, is never
adequate.

We can imagine the compelling presence of Jesus as He
rises to address the congregation. His only vestments are a
penetrating gaze and a captivating eloquence. Either reading
from a scroll (such as was delivered to Him another day in the
Nazareth synagogue) or quoting from memory, Jesus
"preached the word unto them" (Mark 2:2 KJV). We don't
know His text, but we can be sure that the Word of Life
became alive to His congregation.

Long-suffering laypersons who Sunday after Sunday
endure poor to mediocre preaching surely have my sympathy.
They deserve better than that! Sermons *can* be rich in
content—scriptural exposition, relevant illustrations, insightful quotations, and pictorial phrases that weave a common
thread throughout the message. Sermons *can* be delivered in
such a way as to focus attention upon the speaker instead of
on the number of panels in the chancel. Sermons *can* sound
the positive notes of redemption, hope, and love.

Every year I spend at least a couple of days at a black
campmeeting. Most black preachers know how to keep their

110

congregations awake. They preach with enthusiasm. They use colorful language. And they get down to cases. Of course, they also preach to very responsive audiences. That always helps even the poorest of preachers!

Laypersons come to worship expecting to hear some fresh word from God. Throughout the week, Dan Rather has presented the news professionally prepared and up to the minute. Expectations are the same for the preacher. The Good News deserves at least as much preparation as the bad news.

Doberstein (Thielicke's translator) writes, "What I and many of my colleagues hear . . . is that people want good preaching. Again and again, highly intellectual lay people, who love the church and the Lord of the church, say to us, 'Why can't we have better preaching?' "[5] Doberstein continues, "Wherever we find, even in this day, a vital, living congregation we find at its center vital preaching."[6] Elton Trueblood adds, "There have been no changes in our culture which alter the fact that the spoken word may be a powerful force in human life."[7]

A commitment to excellence in preaching makes two assumptions: (1) that Scripture is capable of profoundly influencing those who hear it, and (2) that preaching can be a powerful way of presenting Scripture. The Bible itself supports both assumptions. It pleases God "by the folly of what we preach to save those who believe" (1 Cor. 1:21). Furthermore, the gospel "is the power of God unto salvation to everyone that believeth" (Rom. 1:16 KJV). Like twin pillars, neither of these Pauline professions can be removed or even weakened without causing the roof to topple in upon the blind man who desecrates them.

Dr. Wallace Fisher states the preacher's position this way, "Called to be a colaborer with Christ, he places his confidence in the gospel of God and the human activity of preaching. Lack of confidence in either maims the church's exercise of Christ's ministry. Let any ordained minister of Christ's church come before the tribunal of biblical evidence to get his bearings if he does not believe that God was in

111

Christ, that scriptures witness to that mighty deed, and that preaching is a primary means for communicating this good news to man."[8]

Anyone who advises a pastor to neglect the pulpit in favor of other ministries is to that pastor what Simon Peter was to Jesus when he sought to deter Jesus from going to Jerusalem. "Get thee behind me, Satan," is the only proper response to any such advice. Preaching is as much God's way as the cross was God's way. Preaching apart from the Bible reduces the preacher's effort to human striving and his message to earthly knowledge. Conversely, without the preacher, the Bible is a priceless coin lost in an ecclesiastical ghetto.

While it must never be assumed that God uses preaching no matter how poor, simply because He has chosen to rely so heavily upon it, preaching does have a mystical cast that strongly suggests divine attachment. Merrill Abbey declares, "Any adequate theology of preaching builds on the conviction that God not only commissions and sends preachers; he is himself present in true preaching."[9] P. T. Forsyth went so far as to intimate that there is a "sacramental quality" to a sermon.[10]

112

A homiletics professor of mine once said, "Preaching that starts in the Bible and stays in the Bible is not biblical preaching." His rationale was that the great preachers of the Bible—the prophets and Jesus—did not just quote Scripture but drew heavily on contemporary illustrations. That is undeniably true. Yet preaching scarce on Scripture is scarce on divine inspiration, even if it is an inspiring message. God's messenger will not draw his major thought from the dust of classical literature or the ashes of today's headlines. Instead, he will resort to, "Thus saith the Lord."

Mark informs us that "Jesus came . . . preaching the gospel" (Mark 1:14). Any pastor who wants a full house had better follow his Lord's example.

The second attraction of the service in Capernaum was the preeminence of Christ. He *was* the service. Without Him worship would have amounted to no more than the lifeless gatherings of the Pharisees. Everyone's attention was drawn to Him. In fact, the crowd had gathered because of the news that He was in the house. Christ's presence always makes a building a sanctuary.

The most uplifting worship services are those in which Jesus Christ is praised. Nothing enables sitting together in heavenly places like the exaltation of our risen Lord. Nothing bids the timid heart to speak like the nearness of Jesus. When Christ presides over a worship service, it takes on the note of victory. It is as if He calls our names the way He called Mary's as she sought Him in the garden.

Whenever called upon to pray publicly, a friend of mine invariably begins, "Dear Jesus . . . " I suspect he does the same in his private prayers. None of this "O thou who in thy mightiness dost look down from heaven upon us with feignless pity. . . " for this humble child of God. Suddenly he has made us all feel right at home in God's house. Project the image of a dour, distant, dreaded deity upon a congregation, and even the called become frozen. Worship that values dignity above all else serves only the ascetic taste of the worship leader. In the family of God there is freedom of expression, just as there is in every happy home.

I have heard worship theorists refer to Isaiah 6 as their textbook for worship. Personally, I prefer Mark 2. If we could reproduce Isaiah's experience each Sunday morning at 11:00 so that everyone "saw the Lord sitting upon a throne, high and lifted up," we might empty, rather than fill our churches. Ah, but if we could duplicate the experience in the little house in Capernaum, we would have overflow crowds every Sunday. Most of us find God most personable in the person of Jesus Christ. God's charm is not His "train that fills the temple," but Jesus' smile that floods our souls. "High and lifted up" is not for most of us. We need to know that our God is "meek and lowly in heart." The most universal symbol of acceptance in all the world is the figure of Jesus standing with arms outstretched saying, "Come to me, all who labor and are heavy laden" (Matt. 11:28).

113

Charles Wesley understood how important the preeminence of Christ is to worship when he wrote,

*O for a thousand tongues to sing
My great Redeemer's praise,
The glories of my God and King,
The triumphs of His grace!*

Because God has cloaked Himself in the form of a lowly Nazarene we dare to "come boldly unto the throne of grace, that we may obtain mercy" (Heb. 4:16 KJV). Adam and Eve fled from the awesomeness of God following their sin. Conversely, a woman of the streets burst in as an unwelcome guest in order to be near Jesus. Jesus appeals to both saints and sinners. People still come to church with the age-old request, "Sir, we wish to see Jesus" (John 12:21).

There was a third significant thing about the service in Capernaum. There was action! God's power was asserted in a demonstration of His mighty works. Having great faith in the healing ministry of Christ, several men brought a friend who was afflicted with palsy. Finding no way to get through the throng in the house, they climbed to the roof, removed several tiles, and lowered their friend on a stretcher right into the Lord's presence. Jesus was greatly impressed with their faith and responded by instantly healing the man. Can you imagine what this turn of events would do to a printed order of worship?

Predictability is deadening to worship. I listened one time as members of a large Sunday school class discussed the pros and cons of structured worship. Some complained that the worship services of their church always followed the same order. Some lamented the loss of freedom in their worship. One or two longed for the good old days when "amens" were heard throughout the sanctuary. Anything that inhibits participation in worship—whether it be an established order of worship, tight control by the worship leader, or threatening stares from fellow worshipers—makes worship less alive, and hence less inviting.

114

My wife and I encountered a little church in a Montana mountain community where, prior to the regular worship hour, a layperson displayed words to contemporary gospel music using an overhead projector. The congregation sang these songs lustily, a pleasing complement to the traditional hymns that were sung later.

Skilled worship leaders are not *performers;* they are *orchestraters.* That is, they facilitate worship by encouraging people to be involved and by evoking response from them. People want to participate in worship and to express what they are feeling. Only when spontaneity is encouraged can the Lord do His mighty works among us. What happened in Capernaum can happen in our churches if we are open to it.

Spontaneity, of course, must always comply with the apostle Paul's admonition, "all things should be done decently and in order" (1 Cor. 14:40). Let those who would exercise freedom in worship say and do only that which edifies. Exhibitionism has no place in worship; nor does monopolizing the time or haranguing. Freedom in worship should not be construed as license to disrupt.

I was once in a meeting with several hundred ministers and their wives in which the Spirit of God was unusually present. Inspiration was at high tide. In the middle of a song we were singing everyone in the balcony spontaneously stood up. The worship leader immediately acknowledged it and bade the rest of us to rise to our feet. It was the nearest thing I have ever seen to a wave in a worship service.

115

Follow the crowds and you will see that they are going where things are happening, and not just the routine things either. We all want to sense the Spirit of God moving on the face of the deep. We want God to act again. We want to relive creation. We want there to be light!

They raised the roof in Capernaum. Are we trying to keep the lid on worship?

12
The Family
as Good Neighbors

One year my wife served as the official chaperon for Miss Indiana as she traveled about the state to make public appearances for a number of events and gatherings. During this time their casual acquaintance developed into a genuine friendship. Terry was a special person. In addition to having physical beauty and considerable talent, she was a true Christian. Her father was a physician; her grandfather a minister. She sometimes sang for us at the church were I was the pastor.

Even though Terry was born with the proverbial silver spoon in her mouth, her orientation was to service. In the lounge of the rest room of a large sports complex a small concession stand offered toiletries and personal hygiene products. She did not need to make a purchase, yet Terry paused to talk several minutes with the woman who operated the concession—not as a celebrity, but as one human being to another. That she had as much time for obscure people as for important people really qualified her to wear her crown.

The family of God does not exist in a vacuum. It exists in a very real world. God has intended that it be so. Members of the family of God are expected to be good neighbors—reaching out to those around them, loving them and caring for their needs. The family of God must never be conceived of as a closed group of people who are concerned only with each other and with getting to heaven.

Sometimes a congregation whose house of worship is surrounded by poverty, injustice, physical abuse, or moral degradation has no intentional ministry to its own neighborhood. That congregation may boast about how pure its members are, how "spiritual" its services of worship are, how many people attend the Wednesday evening prayer meeting, and how much money it sends to the mission field. Yet, *that* family of God is *not* a good neighbor. Good neighbors get involved in the plight of those around them. *That* congregation is no better than the priest and the Levite who passed by on the other side when they saw the man who had fallen among thieves (Luke 10:30–37).

Being a good neighbor means little things like giving a smile or five minutes of undivided time to a lonely widow. It means showing acceptance and understanding for a rebellious and wayward young person. It means helping a man who is down on his luck rather than ignoring the need. Good neighbors express their religion through caring as well as through worship. They practice their religion where they live, work, purchase, and play, as well as in the church building where they meet.

Being a lover of old cars, I once purchased a 1963 Ford Galaxie from a widow in our congregation. The interior of the car looked almost new, but the paint was faded and rust spots had developed. So I took it to the body shop for repairs. How happy I was when I picked up my new toy two days before Christmas. Off I drove into the dark, heading for home ten miles away. One minor concern disturbed my euphoria: the fuel gauge did not work. Sure enough, the motor soon sputtered and died. Ruefully, I pulled off to the side of the road. The prospects of finding a gas station were bleak as I got out of the car into the bitter cold and began to run. Anxiety and the brisk air fed energy into my body. Not far ahead of me, perhaps a half mile on the left, loomed the lights of a Phillips 66 station. What a welcome sight! Would they have a gas can to loan? I wondered.

My thoughts were interrupted as a luxury van pulled

alongside me and stopped. The driver beckoned me to climb on board. Another welcome sight! Entering a world of warmth and comfort, I explained my embarrassing predicament. He drove me to the station, helped me secure a small container of gasoline, and graciously insisted on driving me back to my car. As I poured the gas into the tank he stood patiently at my side, then waited as I tried to restart the engine. Despite some tantalizing chugs, the motor would not run, even though we had poured a little fuel directly into the carburetor.

Not knowing what else to do, we returned to the gas station for more fuel. By now I was really feeling like a pain in the neck, especially when I overheard my helper phone his wife to say that she should go on to the party without him; he would be there as soon as he could. Back to my car we went to repeat the entire operation. This time, praise the Lord, my car started. With profound appreciation I thanked my rescuer for his timely assistance. During the forty-five minutes we had spent together I had learned that this very special person was an active Christian. He was a member of the family of God, and a great neighbor! How easy it would have been to have "passed by on the other side." In spite of the reasons why he might not have stopped, he *did* stop. Caring compelled him to.

Speaking of gas stations, I know at least one owner who is interested in more than just profit. This very able business woman, who is a committed Christian, cares about people. When an unemployed minister and his wife took refuge in our city, she hired both of them. They were coming off a painful experience and really needed to leave the stress of pastoring for a little while. Knowing that these two employees would not likely stay long enough to make a lasting contribution to her business did not deter this woman from hiring them, as it would have many employers. She is a member of the family of God, and a great neighbor!

At about that time two delightful young families affiliated with the congregation of which I was then the pastor. One of the men was a pediatrician who had come to our city to enter practice with his brother. The other had moved to our

119

community to take a sales executive position. Both men joined our sanctuary choir. One evening the doctor learned that the salesman had purchased an old house near the church and was in the process of remodeling it. This had proved to be a major undertaking threatening to take many months if the man worked at the job alone as he had been doing. The doctor, an able carpenter, recruited a helper or two and volunteered to assist in the remodeling. Over the next several weeks the doctor and the salesman, though coming from very different backgrounds, spent many pleasant hours together sawing boards and driving nails. The finished product was not only a lovely home but a deep friendship between the two families. The doctor had learned from his minister father that being a member of the family of God means being a good neighbor.

The secretary of a pulpit committee contacted me to secure names of prospective pastors. In the process of describing her congregation to me, she listed the occupations of several members, told me something of their approach to ministry, and identified the gifts they desired most in their next pastor. However, I was most impressed by a story she told me. Twins had recently been born to a young couple in the congregation. One had a defective heart, necessitating immediate surgery. The other suffered from a serious breathing disorder requiring additional medical attention. Members of the congregation moved quickly to be of support, giving time and money, bringing in food, and praying earnestly for recovery of the newborns. It was easy for me to send names to that congregation. What minister would not wish to pastor such a caring group?

Beware lest you make doing good your religion, or feel self-righteous because you pour oil on wounds instead of praying on the street corner. The priest and the Levite had no time for human need. But what of good neighbors who have no time for the temple? While a true member of God's family is concerned about being a neighbor, that person also cherishes relationships within the family and joins them regularly to worship God from whom all righteousness comes.

Members of the family of God should often be benefactors, but, like the rest of society, we are also debtors. That by itself should save us from feelings of self-righteousness.

I listen with interest to the monologues my dentist seems to perform so effortlessly whenever he has his fist in my mouth. While he repaired a molar recently, he chose to tell me about a benefactor who years ago had paid his way through dental school. "That," he commented, "is a debt I am going to have to repay one of these days." My dentist feels an obligation to help some deserving young man or woman through dental school, just as he was helped.

It is a mark of character to remember that one is a debtor, and to do something about it. Think for just a moment about those key persons who in one way or another have helped you along the journey of life. You, too, are a debtor. Right?

Members of the family of God should be especially conscious of their debts. As recipients of God's grace we should remain forever humble and thankful. What is more natural than for Christians to give themselves in service to others in appreciation for the blessings they enjoy through Jesus Christ? Members of the family of God should be the greatest neighbors in the world, always ready to help whatever the need. That means that the local congregation will need to program to meet human needs in the community and around the world. It also means that individual Christians will need to be alert to opportunities to help, as was the Good Samaritan the day he traveled from Jerusalem to Jericho.

121

13
The Pastor
and His Roles

Like the sun's rays streaming through a stained-glass window, the pastor's personality colors the people in the pews. If his attitude is positive and his disposition warm, the congregation will take on the amber glow of contentment. If his spirit is dark and his temperament mean, the church will be overcast with a sullen haze. That his influence should be so profound is inescapable. By virtue of his very position he cannot be other than the key to his congregation's happiness or unhappiness.

As a father does for a family, the pastor sets the mood in the church. If he is explosive, retaliatory, suspicious, judgmental, or authoritarian, he will eventually have that kind of congregation. If he is gentle and kind, slow to anger and plenteous in mercy; if he is moderate and democratic, trusting and fair, in time the whole church will take on his likeness.

Someone has said that after five years a pastor's problems are his own creation. A pastor's sins and neuroses, like those of any progenitor, are visited upon the third and fourth generations. A problem church has probably been a problem church for years (at least off and on). The likelihood is that a pastor injured the fellowship several decades ago by impropriety or indiscretion. Every succeeding pastor has to reap a little of the whirlwind sown by his distant predecessor.

But this can be changed! The present pastor must be an amber window, imperturbably streaming golden rays of love until the last dark shadow has vanished. It may take more than five years, but it can be done. A succession of short pastorates won't do it. Nor will it be accomplished by an autocrat whose Messiah complex compels him to stay until every last "troublemaker" has been cremated or driven from the camp. One man—stout of heart, sound of mind, firm of purpose, and above all, permeated by Christ's love—can transform a disgruntled congregation into a vital church.

A certain church had been torn asunder by a series of unfortunate incidents extending over several pastorates. Called to this scene was a man of wisdom and godly love. Although limited in formal training, his gentle manner brought healing to troubled spirits. He pastored there for twelve years, and when he left, it could be said of that congregation, "Behold, how they love one another." His successor, received with open arms, inherited a tremendous wealth of goodwill that had been built up over those twelve years. What a difference one amber window can make!

What are we saying? Simply that the deeply happy church begins with a genuinely happy pastor. Let's not oversimplify what happiness is. It is not enough that the pastor be happy when he is preaching, or happy when he is playing golf, or happy because of a raise in salary, or happy because the attendance was good last Sunday. This will not necessarily edify the complexion of his church. He will produce a happy church only if he is *at heart a happy man.*

This brings us to a discussion of the pastor's emotional stability. Few professions are inclined to be more trauma-producing than the pastoral ministry. The pastoral ministry is no place for the maladjusted. The man who comes to this calling needs emotional balance, or as psychologists call it, ego strength. If he is not at heart a secure man, he will become increasingly an insecure pastor. The ministry seems to exploit every personality weakness. A person might have a dozen hang-ups and still function quite well as an accountant or farmer, but almost every kink (or bend) in a minister's thinking will militate against his effectiveness. If his emotional security is impaired to any degree, this may precipitate a crisis in his church or make it impossible for him to survive a crisis arising from other causes.

The pastor who contributes to a well-balanced church preserves the peace, whereas a less composed pastor might trigger, by his reaction, a chain of reactions among the people. A peaceful church is the expressed solitude of its pastor's soul. Pastors should be shock absorbers, not vibrators. A pastor who is easily threatened will be a vibrator. One who is not easily threatened will be a shock absorber.

Rev. Alonzo pastored several congregations, trouble arising in each. In his last charge he acted as chairman of the board of trustees. He refused to allow his youth director to conduct youth meetings without his presence, and even insisted on attending every meeting of the women's society. Underneath this strange mode of operation was an over-whelming sense of insecurity, the obsession, "they are out to get me." Inevitably his hyper-suspicion fractured relationships in the congregation and led to his ouster. While this is an extreme example, it does illustrate the disaster that can result when a pastor begins to act out of fear, feeling that either his reputation or position is in jeopardy.

125

The secure pastor has confidence in himself, faith in God, and a great trust in God's people. He is not always reading something into words said or things done by members of his congregation, particularly those who are influential. He is not jealous of those within his congregation who are admired. He is not fearful of those whose power could be used to challenge his own. He does not interpret disagreement with his ideas, criticism of his sermon, or exclusion from a small group get-together as personal rejection.

The secure pastor does not have to be praised excessively in order to feel his ministry is appreciated. He is comfortable with his people. Because he is not up-tight, they relax around him. A feeling is transmitted throughout the fellowship, "Our pastor accepts us. We accept him."

THE PASTOR'S ROLES

As the pastor functions in the several roles integral to his assignment, he should assume a posture that will prompt a positive response from members of the congregation. It may be helpful to contrast the options open to the pastor as he alternately functions as teacher, preacher, pastor, and leader.

Teacher: Model Not Master

If the pastor asks, "How can I best impart knowledge and understanding to my people?" he may wish to consider the following premises: (1) adults do not receive information uncritically, and (2) examples are more convincing than words. If these two statements are true, the answer to the question becomes more obvious.

Most people who sit in the pew will neither accept as fact nor abide by as commandment what the teacher says simply because he stands behind "the sacred desk." Therefore the pastor will not find it particularly effective to make unsupported declarations. Even if he selects some random proof texts to support his case and pounds the pulpit to emphasize it, thinking persons will remain unimpressed. "Says who?" or "Says you!" will be their mental response.

What will impress students is solid evidence that, although the teacher knows his subject, he does not consider himself the final authority. He will provide substantial content on the subject, but he will also leave ample room for his listeners to process his message through their own intellect and to enhance it with their own insights. To talk down to or demean an audience by outlawing dissent insults their intelligence. The pastor must try to stimulate as well as to inform. To the degree that his listeners feel a partnership with him in the discovery of truth, they will be active listeners. Only active listeners are learners.

If laypeople are to be adequately nurtured in the Christian faith, they need more than stimulation. They also need simulation. Intellectual discoveries must find embodiment. It is imperative for the pastor to serve as an example, reproducing the life of Christ before his people. He must rely less and less upon dogmatic pronouncements from the pulpit and more and more upon his own conduct to communicate the gospel. The pastor is not likely to be accepted as master (as Jesus was by His disciples), but he will readily be accepted as model. What he cannot command with words he can constrain with deeds. If his people see demonstrated in the pastor love, holiness, servanthood, peace, and joy, they are far more likely to seek these qualities than if he merely speaks of them as being highly desirable. Furthermore, as the emergence of these qualities becomes evident in the pastor's life, each will seem within reach of the laity.

The pastor is called upon to model not so much a finished product as an ongoing process. No one is more pretentious than the person who claims to have fully attained Christian perfection. No one is more admired and emulated than one who is distinctively Christian, yet quick to confess that there is plenty of room for improvement. Thus, the pastor will model humility as well as holiness, sorrow as well as joy, uncertainty as well as certainty. If the people are to identify with him, the pastor must be a becomer among becomers and a learner among learners.

127

One of the most successful pastors I have ever observed was not highly educated. The phrase I most commonly associate with his ministry is, "I don't know. . . ." However, that dear brother made us all feel like he was one of us. When he shared a revelation from God we eagerly received it as a gift from one human being to another. His Christian pilgrimage was so exciting we were enticed to go along with him.

Preacher: Activator Not Agitator

We all know that the standard form of communication is dialogue, not monologue. Why, then, do people subject themselves to sitting on hard pews to listen to twenty- to forty-minute sermons? It does seem rather incredible that literally millions of people do so every Sunday, especially since many sermons are downright dull. What is the pastor's best stewardship of the time his flock has so graciously allocated to him?

The preacher may elect to tell his listeners how terrible they are. He will not need much imagination to convince either himself or them of this. Furthermore, any pastor worthy of his calling will be compelled to reprove sin. He will occasionally find it timely to call for repentance. When done in season and in good taste this kind of preaching receives favorable response. Indeed, preaching can only be respected when it is true to *all* of the gospel, including the note of judgment.

However, the preacher must ultimately decide whether his prevailing stance will be positive or negative. If he consistently castigates his flock, he will have assumed the role of agitator whether he realizes it or not. A steady diet of hell fire and brimstone eventually turns people upon the preacher and against one another. It establishes a critical tone throughout the congregation. Each person becomes a judge armed with Scripture to cite as a law that has been broken.

The preacher cannot demand conformity to God's commandments. Consistently attempting to do so will only make his hearers defensive. Defensive people are not good listeners. Anger blocks out the message no matter how valid it may be. Recently I was looking over an old church directory and discovered that sometime in the years past it had fallen into the hands of my young son. In cartoon fashion he had added words to several of the photographs in keeping with poignant facial expressions. Of course my picture was at the front of the directory. It was a large picture, snapped while I was delivering a sermon. To the picture my son had added these words, "All right, you turkeys, shape up or ship out." I was not amused by this portrayal. Such ineptitude only results in futility.

Does this take the role of prophet and evangelist away

from the pastor? By no means. Just as people are willing to learn if their own intelligence is respected, so they are willing to improve if their worth is acknowledged. Most people generally don't want to be told what truth is. They prefer to be facilitated in its discovery. Rather than to be told what is wrong with them, they prefer to be led in self-examination. When the preacher is able to inspire people to live more nobly than they ever dreamed possible, he is an activator. We do want to be inspired. We are eager to believe that we can change. Too bad if there is more inspiration at Weight Watchers than at church.

Pastor: Advocate Not Adversary

Jesus spoke of himself as the Good Shepherd who gave His life for His sheep. Paul commended that model to those who would follow him as pastor of the church at Ephesus. Clearly the biblical image of the pastor is that of advocate, not that of adversary. We have little trouble with this in theory, but we have considerable trouble with it in practice.

The pastor may drift or be thrust into the adversarial role without his intention, and against his will. It is terrifying, sometimes paralyzing, to sense a rift developing between oneself and influential members of the congregation and being powerless to prevent it. Ministers often sit in my office and discuss this mystery. "How can this be happening to me?" they ask.

Sometimes pastors who feel pushed toward an adversarial position actually make matters worse. By their own defense mechanisms and/or political tactics they accelerate the mounting tension. The most natural tendency when finding oneself at odds with certain members of the congregation is to panic. Panic responses are seldom constructive. Sometimes pastors try to avoid those who see them as adversaries, staying out of their presence as much as possible. This passive response can be interpreted as a slight. A more aggressive response is an attempt to isolate the troubling members, to discredit their character, their wisdom, or their spirituality, to unseat them from positions of leadership if possible. Such tactics only enlarge the adversary image.

To prevent adversarial relationships and to cultivate the role of advocacy, one must be intentional, charitable, and vulnerable. Being intentional, he will go to those from whom he is growing apart and practice the ounce of prevention in lieu of a pound of cure. Being charitable, he will think the best of all others even when evidence is alarming. Being vulnerable, he will communicate his concern, his willingness to be corrected, and his openness to negotiation. By hearing others out, and not discrediting either them or their case, the sting can be taken out of the conflict.

How is it that even the pastor who knows better sometimes finds himself in an adversarial relationship with certain members of the congregation? The explanations are complex and numerous. Basically they can be encompassed in four words: propositions, principles, projects, and plans.

Propositions. Here the issue is, "What shall we believe?" We do not all believe the same thing even about the essentials of the faith. We have differing interpretations of just what was "delivered unto the saints." Pastors may take doctrinal or theological positions contrary to "in house" understandings. Certainly that is the pastor's option, but if he elects to do so he may be saddled with the role of adversary. Say the pastor disagrees with certain tenets that are held by members of the congregation. If he makes this known, he may be attacked as a threat to orthodoxy, or he may elect to go on the offensive by attempting to "straighten out" those who are "misled."

Only as the pastor is willing to dialogue rather than discredit will he be able to escape the role of adversary. His task is not to prove anyone wrong. He is there to protect the right of his people to discover truth. That is an advocacy position. Hence, the pastor must honor the views of others, setting forth his own views in a way that does not quench conviction but invites reconsideration. When issues such as abortion, glossolalia, and eschatology threaten to divide us, the pastor must be a bridge-builder, not a wall-builder. He needs to be an advocate on the behalf of each person in the congregation regardless of differences in opinion.

Principles. Here the issue is, "How shall we live as believers?" Feelings run high among committed Christians about what is acceptable and what is not acceptable behavior. As chief spokesperson for the "right," the pastor can easily become the adversary of those who "come short." Some will even pressure him to preach condemnatory sermons. Yet, the pastor must be the advocate of all persons, especially sinners. While never condoning sin, he will remember that those who feel he is set against them will not likely seek him. Opportunities for ministry come to advocates, not adversaries. Sometimes a pastor may find it necessary to reproach, but most of the time he will find it wiser to coach. In either case, he must do it with love.

Projects. Here the issue is, "What shall be our mission as a church?" I have observed that more pastors get into adversarial positions with their people over congregational objectives than over any other single factor. A leader always runs the risk of facing opposition. When pastors insist on ramming their plans through, while key laypersons insist that it shall not be done, opposition can become intense. If the pastor brands his opponents as obstructionists, he has clearly identified himself as an adversary.

131

Deciding what God has called our congregation to be about is something we do together. People have ideas and concerns of their own, and they wish for those ideas and concerns to be respected. They also stand most ready to give their full support to their own ideas and concerns and not necessarily to the plans and concerns of the pastor.

Plans. Here the issue is, "How shall we accomplish what we have jointly decided to do?" Sometimes it is easier to agree on objectives than on strategies. A pastor who begins to boss people around will soon become their adversary. If instead, he enables them to do careful planning and supports them as they carry out plans, he will be cherished as an advocate.

Anxious pastors are usually perceived as adversaries, not advocates. They are so fearful of failure they cannot trust others to do their work right. Self-promoting pastors are jealous of plans, lest somehow there will come a slip-up. Hence they must hover over all board and committee meetings to insure that the right decisions are made. Pastors who use their people to make them look good usually come across as adversaries, not advocates, because they exert so much influence in planning and so much pressure in executing. No wonder so many pastors leave within a year after a new building is constructed. In volunteer organizations—and that includes the church—diligence does not result from being driven. It results from being equipped. Equipping is advocacy. Equippers make others look good.

A friend of mine recently celebrated twenty years as pastor of a superb midwestern congregation. Would you believe that it is his first charge? Would you believe that before his arrival that church had run off one pastor after another in short order? They said he would never make it. Some perhaps still believe he lacks humility and tact. Give him credit! During those twenty years there has not been one major schism in the church. Some pastors stay by surviving one civil war after another. Not this pastor. He has stayed because he is an advocate of his people, not an adversary. He brags on them shamelessly. He has led them in major building programs and in nearly two decades of annual faith promise conventions and other unprecedented outreach giving. He has attracted and enjoyed the loyalty of a succession of outstanding associate ministers. How? By being an affirmer of all who surround him. Affirming is advocacy.

Propositions and principles relate almost exclusively to the shepherding role of the pastor. Projects and plans demonstrate whether the pastor is an advocate or adversary in his role as leader.

Leader: Catalyst Not Commander

No one can lead from the adversary position. Only advocates lead. Remember, an advocate is someone who respects the views of others, who is redemptive toward those who have gone astray, who invites the ideas of others, and who facilitates those who are on mission. Such a person has so endeared himself to members of his congregation that they are eager to follow him. He has amassed a store of goodwill that he can expend in a call for cooperation and dedication. Yet he will draw only sparingly on those accumulated credits. Mostly, he will be a generator of ideas, a dreamer of dreams. He will share his ideas and dreams but not press inordinately for their adoption. He may be a major contributor to the congregational "think tank" but he should not consider himself the only contributor. As other ideas and dreams are seriously considered the pastor must be impartial to his own. As the mind of Christ becomes clear in each matter the pastor acts as catalyst, not commander. He gathers the people together in support of great ideas and compelling causes. He focuses their attention on the worthy and the unifying. He inspires to action. He is the servant leader who has no aspirations except to see the church prosper, no agenda except the will of God. He leads in commitment but will not prescribe the commitment of others. He gives guidance but does not demand followership.

One of my favorite people is a distinguished but lively retiree. He pastored for many years, sometimes in easy places and sometimes in hard ones. He was successful wherever he served. Perhaps his most shining accomplishment was taking a church that had bitterly parted company with a previous pastor and developing it into a fine congregation. He felt they needed to relocate and build a new building and he led them to purchase a choice piece of land on the outskirts of the city. Although his people loved him greatly, he met resistance when he proposed construction. He accepted their reticence and respected their internal timetable. Shortly after his successor's arrival the congregation built a beautiful new edifice. It is no less a tribute to the leadership of the pastor who presided over its construction than to the pastor who led them to readiness.

Blessed are those who plant and water and do not tear up and destroy. Because of them the increase comes.

14
Enlarging the Family

Plenty of room in the family,
Room for the young and the old;
Plenty of happiness, plenty of love;
Plenty of room in the fold.[11]

Jesus intended the family of God to be a growing one, for He left us with this Great Commission, "Go therefore and make disciples of all nations, baptizing them in the name of the Father and of the Son and of the Holy Spirit" (Matt. 28:19). It is not by the will of men that there is room in the family (although we may freely concur). It is by the will of God. The inclusiveness of the family is not a sociological inclination so much as it is a theological imperative. As surely as God added to the family on the day of Pentecost, His sovereignty over the church still guarantees a place for all who believe on His name. A local congregation from which any true child of God can be excluded is a secular organization, a social clique, or both. It is not the family of God.

Having described the church in ideal terms, we must admit that local congregations may exist to which strangers— at least certain strangers—are not welcome. The rejection may come as formal denial of membership or as a cold shoulder. In either case, the newcomer understands that he or she doesn't fit in. The reasons local congregations are not open to certain persons are numerous, but all are a denial of the nature of the family of God.

Sometimes we try to protect the close fellowship we have in the church. It is natural for established groups to be closed. Over a period of time, trust develops among the members, bonds of love are formed, understandings are negotiated. The presence of outsiders will inevitably disturb the equilibrium of the group. As one woman said to her pastor, "We don't want a lot of new people coming in here and spoiling the family feelings we have in our church." Even in the church the tendency to limit membership should be seen as more *natural* than *carnal*.

Sometimes our resistance to newcomers is largely ego-centered—an attempt to protect territory we have claimed for ourselves and have no intentions of sharing without a fight. Seldom do we hear anyone confess that he is jealous of his or her power in the church. Nonetheless, one of the most common conflicts in local congregations is that between the "pioneers" and the "homesteaders." Although this is an ideological conflict to the degree that the two groups have differing views about how the church is to be run, it is most typically a conflict over power. At issue is whether those who have seniority in that place are going to move over and make room for the Johnny-come-latelys. The conflict surfaces when the "homesteaders" are expected to share leadership positions with the "pioneers." Plenty of room in the family? Not if a newcomer is going to take my place on the board of deacons.

Sometimes we are not so much protecting power as prominence. Plenty of room in the family? Not if I am going to lose my place on the piano bench.

Obviously if our heavenly Father is to be well pleased with the family of God we must overcome our provincialism and pride. Our primary energies must be directed not toward protecting membership in the family, but toward enlarging the family. The principle mission of the New Testament church was to evangelize.

The happiest experiences in the Huttenlocker household have been those two occasions when increases came to our family. How my wife and I rejoiced when on March 2, 1956, a son was born to us, and again on January 30, 1962, when another boy arrived.

Nothing could be more natural than rejoicing over an enlarged family circle. Our experience certainly is not unique. Each new member of the family means another life to whom we can give love and from whom we can receive love. The whole creation stems from our heavenly Father's very own desire to share relationships with other living souls. This is exemplified in the Garden of Eden.

The same principle applies to the church. The family of God is never happier than when new members are added. The church knows no greater morale booster than a birth announcement. Every time a Nicodemus comes to Jesus, if God's people know anything about it, there is great rejoicing.

Paul and Barnabas had been commissioned as missionaries and went forth with great success evangelizing the Gentiles. Conversions, in fact, were so many that it became necessary to inform the church in Jerusalem just exactly what was happening out on the mission field. So Paul and Barnabas took a furlough. As they journeyed to the council meeting, they visited Phenice and Samaria. There in Christian assemblies they reported the results of their labors like missionaries do today. This news "gave great joy to all the brethren" (Acts 15:3).

137

We are told that the angels in heaven rejoice over one soul that repents. In this the church has the advantage. Angels can only observe each blessed event, but God's people may actually assist in the process. Samuel Wolcott said it well when he wrote: "Christ for the world we sing; the world to Christ we bring, with joyful song: the new born souls whose days, reclaimed from error's ways, inspired with hope and praise, to Christ belong."

The family of God must learn to *think* evangelistically. The great preoccupation of its people is to reach out and bring others to Christ. Soul winning is preeminent in the talk of the church, whether in formal planning or in informal conversation.

During a week as guest of a Christian businessman I accompanied him on several occasions as he went about his work. Business was his topic of conversation from the time he arose in the morning until he retired in the evening. It was easy for me to tell where his heart was. With much apparent satisfaction he spoke of the deals he had completed in the past, those presently being consummated, and others he contemplated closing in the future. Perhaps it took that singleness of purpose to bring him success. Certainly he had done well. This sort of wholehearted devotion is also found among those most successful in bringing others to Christ. They too are obsessed with a purpose.

It is not surprising that some churches seldom see conversions in their midst. While this businessman—thoroughly schooled in Evangelical theology and himself a product of the born-again way—was doing well for himself, he was utterly failing Christ. He was neglecting his first responsibility as a Christian: that of witnessing.

When a majority of those within a congregation become preoccupied with their own private affairs, evangelism inevitably suffers. Outreach breaks down. The aim of the church is not refuted; it is simply brushed aside. Soul-winning becomes the other fellow's business. Thus, the church is the victim of a corrosive, secularizing process.

There is little hope that any church will find joy apart from a passion for souls. The congregation whose fellowship has become listless, impersonal, perhaps even ill-tempered, can best be transformed by a new mind-set, the same one that motivated Paul and Barnabas.

During a series of evangelistic services in a southern church, a group of concerned young wives decided they should get together to consider how they might more effectively share Christ with their friends. I was invited to their delicious potluck lunch. These were cultured women whose husbands held high-salaried positions. After we finished eating we had a very stimulating around-the-table discussion about personal witnessing. It was a refreshing departure from the trivia so often heard by evangelists around dinner tables. I firmly believe that great good resulted from that meeting.

The family of God must learn to *function* evangelistically. Talk should turn to action. Once the fellowship dispenses, a great invasion force should be unleashed on the community. Everyday situations can become the context for presentation of the gospel.

What Christians say about Christ through the week largely determines what the world does about Him on Sunday. The congregation that sings about Christ during its worship but then becomes silent about Christ in its confrontation with a pagan society resembles a business with a great amount of interoffice communication, but no salesmen out in the field.

A man once said to his pastor, "Don't talk to me about personal soul-winning. I don't want any part of it. It simply isn't my thing." Then he attended one of the informal evangelistic services that spread over the country during the Asbury revival in 1970. The inspiration of that service completely changed his mind. He saw firsthand what happens to a congregation when great numbers of its people overcome their inhibitions and let the glory of Christ shine through them. The next night he was primed and ready as he reported for the second shift at the factory where he worked. By midnight he had shared the *Four Spiritual Laws* (Campus Crusade) with six co-workers.

One congregation is the salt of the earth. Another is taken with a grain of salt. What is the difference? The former moves out boldly into the world to make Christ known. The latter shrivels timidly within its own confines. One takes seriously the Great Commission. The other only pretends to. One is a radiant church. The other casts about for a source of joy.

Only as believers use every opportunity to witness does the world "take note that they have been with Jesus." It

139

seems that some of us have borrowed from the film makers a system of rating testimonies—for some audiences, but not for others. In an inverted way we have thus made our Lord's name an undesirable word. The intimation is that to speak of Christ makes a person guilty of great indiscretion. Nothing stifles the progress of a church more quickly than for that heresy to spread throughout the fellowship.

Ethel Waters said on a network TV talk show, "Honey, when I get a chance to say a good word for Jesus, that's my thing." The problem in many congregations is that saying a good word for Jesus is just not the thing of enough people.

The joy of reaping cannot be separated from the joy of sowing. We need to convince ourselves that it is a pleasure to share Christ, rather than limiting our joy to those times when we ride the coattails of someone else's faithful witness. As is our experience of joy, so shall be our expression of it. Jesus said, "For out of the abundance of the heart the mouth speaketh" (Matt. 12:34). Perhaps if we had more of the abundance of His grace, we would find it easier to glorify Him.

A college professor and a Christian psychologist were discussing the matter of communicating the pleasure of serving Christ. Said the professor, "I find it a joy to witness to my fellow faculty members. Some of them look at me like I must be joking. To me religion is exciting and joyous."

Members of the vital church are only incidentally concerned about how they appear to others. Their primary concern is to give everyone they meet an opportunity to know and enjoy Christ.

Any church will thrive on evangelism. Additions to the family not only make the church happy, they also make it hardy. The gates of hell turn aside from the congregation whose ranks steadily swell. Satan finds it difficult (if not impossible) to spread discord, lethargy, or apostasy when "the Lord [adds] to the church daily such as should be saved" (Acts 2:47 KJV). Every subversive tactic is trampled beneath the cadenced march of the church.

140

A certain church had been torn by pettiness and strife for years. Then a revival broke out, beginning with the conversion of one or two persons for whom a number of the people had earnestly prayed over a period of time. Soon hearts began to melt. Faults were confessed. Repentance was widespread. Suddenly having your own way was not nearly so important as furthering the church's ministry in that community. Thus has revival cured the ills of many a congregation.

Only those who have participated in a Pentecost can fully understand the joy that goes with it. The contentment and sense of fulfillment have no counterpart in sensual pleasure.

More than once I have driven home after preaching a series of evangelistic meetings almost oblivious to the world around me. There was just such a time in northeast Ohio when the final service had been an especially fitting climax to a wonderful week. The lights of the city faded into the background and the darkness of the countryside enveloped me. Alone with my thoughts, and reliving the ecstasy of past adventure, I became lost in wonder, love, and praise. Before I knew it I had missed a fairly familiar turn and found myself off course. Although I had to drive several miles out of the way and was later than expected in arriving home, it did not matter. My joy was only the longer preserved.

If the church will conscientiously "weep o'er the erring one" and "lift up the fallen," she shall harvest her reward. A congregation having a sense of purpose with an accompanying sense of achievement cannot be anything but contented. The ministry of both pastor and people will be self-authenticating. What the church today needs as much as anything else is a restoration of confidence. The church has been maligned for its hypocrisy, irrelevance, incompetence, and failure. We need a success story to build up our sagging ego.

Nothing helps the church affirm its primacy in God's plan like conversions. If the church can point to lives that have been changed, it most eloquently defends its appointment, illuminates its contribution, and asserts its indestructibility.

If anyone really wants to know, "Can I expect the church to love me?" it is pretty safe to reply, "Yes, you certainly can." Go back with me to a congregation I served a number of years ago. There I will show you a woman who had a shameful reputation in the community. Today she is one of the most active and well-liked women in the church. While we are there, I will show you a man who was once an alcoholic. Today he is an influential member in the congregation. He has taught Sunday school and served as youth leader.

Travel with me to other places and I'll show you a gospel singer, once a drug addict, who felt terribly rejected while in high school and in the military service, whose wife left him, who seemed to fail at everything he tried, yet who has found such love in the church that he now believes in himself. I'll show you a biracial youth who was born in disgrace, deprived of a father, and raised in poverty. The one bright spot in his life was a little mission church in his neighborhood. There he learned that Jesus loved him and he experienced the love of those who ministered in that place. I will show you a man, once an agnostic, who today can scarcely number all the friends he has in the church. And, of course, we could mention the apostle Paul, who actually despised the church. Feared at first, he came to be loved by those whom he had once persecuted.

The ultimate praise for all this goes to Jesus Christ, who makes new creatures out of reprobates. But it is also to the church's credit that these and legions more have been welcomed with open arms into its fellowship.

Plenty of room in the family? Yes indeed!

Notes

1. Words by William J. and Gloria Gaither; music by William J. Gaither. Copyright © 1974 by William J. Gaither. All rights reserved. Used by permission of Gaither Music Company.

2. Samuel M. Shoemaker, *With the Holy Spirit and With Fire* (New York: Harper & Row, 1960), p. 112.

3. Dietrich Bonhoeffer, *Life Together* (New York: Harper & Row, 1976), p. 110.

4. James R. Dolby, *I, Too, Am Man* (Waco, Tex.: Word, 1969), p. 5.

5. Helmut Thielicke, *The Trouble with the Church,* trans. John W. Doberstein (New York: Harper & Row, 1965), p. vii.

6. Ibid.

7. Elton Trueblood, *The Incendiary Fellowship* (New York: Harper & Row, 1967), p. 48.

8. Wallace Fisher, *Preaching and Parish Renewel* (New York: Abingdon, 1966), p. 32.

9. Merrill R. Abbey, *Preaching to the Contemporary Mind* (New York: Abingdon, 1963), p. 35.

10. P. T. Forsyth, *Positive Preaching and the Modern Mind* (Cincinnati: Jennings and Graham, 1907), p. 81.

11. Words by William J. and Gloria Gaither; music by William J. Gaither. Copyright © 1974 by William Gaither. All rights reserved. Used by permission of Gaither Music Company.